HUGH LATIMER

BY

R. M. CARLYLE

AND

A. J. CARLYLE

CHAPLAIN AND LECTURER (LATE FELLOW) OF UNIVERSITY COLLEGE OXFORD,
EXAMINING CHAPLAIN TO THE LORD BISHOP OF WORCESTER

WIPF & STOCK · Eugene, Oregon

Wipf and Stock Publishers
199 W 8th Ave, Suite 3
Eugene, OR 97401

Hugh Latimer
By Carlyle, R. M. and Carlyle, A. J.
ISBN 13: 978-1-5326-7099-2
Publication date 9/25/2018
Previously published by Houghton, Mifflin and Company, 1899

HUGH LATIMER

After the Picture in the National Portrait Gallery, from a photograph by Messrs. Walker & Boutall

PREFACE

IT is difficult to write a life of any of the more important personages of the English Reformation; it is difficult to write without prejudice, and the documents of the last part of the reign of Henry VIII. and of the reign of Edward VI. have not yet been calendared. We have endeavoured to give a brief account of Latimer's life and doings, without attempting to deal in detail with the great critical and controversial questions of the time; some will, no doubt, think this improper, but we should like to point out that Latimer's position in English History is not of the kind to make a life of him a convenient starting-point for a discussion of the complicated circumstances of those times.

We have to express our obligations to Canon Dixon's *History of the Church of England in the Time of the Reformation,* especially for the reign of Edward VI. and Queen Mary. The references to the *State Papers* are to the "Letters and Papers, Foreign and Domestic," of the reign of Henry VIII. References to Latimer's *Sermons* and *Remains* are to the two volumes in the Parker Society's publications. References to Strype's *Memorials* are to the edition of the Clarendon Press, 1822, and to Strype's *Cranmer*, Clarendon Press, 1812. Morice, to whom occasional reference is made (taken from Strype), was at one time secretary to Cranmer, and probably reasonably well acquainted with the circumstances of Latimer's life. Augustine Bernher was a personal servant of Latimer. The references to Foxe are to the edition of the *Acts and Monuments* published by R. B. Seeley and W. Burnside, London, 1838.

LIFE OF LATIMER

CHAPTER I

THE history of the Reformation, especially in England, is the history of one of the most complex movements in the history of Europe. The great changes of the sixteenth century were the results of many forces, closely, no doubt, interrelated, but yet diverse in their character. And yet it is but a superficial judgment which fails to perceive that below all the complex forces of the Reformation there lay one great force,—the force of the revival of religion, a passion which possessed men for the recovery of a more spiritual, and therefore a more free and spontaneous, religious life.

The characters of the men who played the greater parts in this movement are often as perplexing as the movement itself. In England especially they are often interesting, but almost always perplexing, full of ideas and gifted with great qualities; but they lack the direct, straightforward, robust character of the great reformers of Germany and Switzerland. And yet again, it is a hasty and superficial judgment which fails to recognise that these men were profoundly stirred, were full of a genuine zeal for the truth. It is no doubt, however, this very lack of simplicity which throws into greater relief the characters of those few great Englishmen, like Sir Thomas More on the one side and Latimer on the other, whose characters exhibit just those qualities of directness, of straightforward simplicity which we usually miss. It was to these qualities, combined with a rare gift of terse and homely eloquence, that Latimer owed his great influence in the movement of the Reformation in England. He would have been the first to acknowledge that he could lay no claim to the title of an original theological thinker, but he did more than any other to translate the conceptions of the theologians of the Reformation in England into language which could be understood of all men; and the simplicity and dignity of his life and death did more than was done by any other to compel the reverence of Englishmen for the Reformation.

In studying the life of Latimer, we must from the outset bear steadily in mind how very different was the Reformation in England before the great reaction under Mary, from the Reformation settlement under Elizabeth. In the movement before Mary we are compelled to recognise that the aims of the religious and of the political leaders of the country moved upon different lines, on lines which only occasionally were even parallel, and that, properly speaking, no reconciliation between their different aims had been reached, until in the reign of Edward VI. the religious leaders persuaded the political, for the time being, to adopt their views. We must remember, too, that the religious leaders had not precisely the same aims before, as after, the Marian persecution. During the earlier period the influence of Luther and Melancthon is paramount; in the later, we see the natural predominance of the logical if narrow mind of Calvin. The attitude of Cranmer and Latimer is therefore to be distinguished, on the one hand, from the general character of the settlement of religion under Elizabeth, and, on the other, from the systematic and rigorous theology of the majority of the early Elizabethan divines.

Latimer, then, stands for a religious idea, which is not precisely the same as that of the English Church since Elizabeth; his conception of the Reformation is essentially that of a reform in religious practice —the removal of superstitions, the repudiation of a usurped authority on the part of the Bishop of Rome. But the very strength of that conception may have led him to forget that consideration for the natural, because traditional, religious sentiment, and for the natural attachment to traditional forms and customs, which is the great glory of the Elizabethan religious order. He is at once more and less dogmatically Protestant in his attitude—more, for he was in continual conflict with the Roman form of religion in practice and in its organised form; less, for he has no rigorously complete religious theory which he opposes to it.

Like Cranmer himself, Latimer is perpetually moving, his ideas are continually developing, his opposition to the old religion grows continually in intensity, but the opposition is of a different sort from that shown in later days; and for himself, he is concerned with the practical and devotional side of religious life, rather than with the theological.

LIFE OF LATIMER

Little is known about the early life of Latimer. In his sermons he has, fortunately, turned aside from time to time from the direct subject of his discourse and told us a little about himself. He was born at Thurcaston, in Leicestershire, probably about the year 1490.[1] His father, he tells us, " was a yeoman and had no lands of his own, only he had a farm of three or four pound by year at the uttermost, and hereupon he tilled so much as kept half a dozen men. He had walk for a hundred sheep, and my mother milked thirty kine. He was able and did find the king a harness with himself and a horse, while he came to the place that he should receive the king's wages. I can remember that I buckled his harness when he went into Blackheath field. He kept me to school, or else I had not been able to have preached before the King's Majesty now. He married my sisters with five pound or twenty nobles apiece; so that he brought them up in godliness and fear of God. He kept hospitality for his poor neighbours, and some alms he gave to the poor."[2]

He belonged, that is, to that sturdy yeoman class which had been so valuable an element of the English nation, a class which was to suffer more than any other from the tremendous social changes which were impending. In the sermon quoted from, Latimer points out the very different position of a small farmer in the time of his manhood from what it was in his boyhood. His father clearly occupied a position of independence; he was poor, but he could bring up his children in

[1] 1485 is suggested by Mr. Mullinger in his *History of the University of Cambridge.*
[2] *Sermons,* p. 101.

such wise that their future was assured to them, and yet he stinted not in hospitality or almsgiving.

The change to the struggling poverty of his father's successor, noted by Latimer, was partly a consequence of the great growth of the trade in wool and of the growth of a new class of landowners who, having made their money in trade, treated the land merely as a means of commercial profit, and cared very little, if at all, for the small peasants whose well-being depended on the cultivation of the soil, and whose condition was miserably depressed by its conversion to mere pasturage. This was one of the evils to which Latimer recurred again and again in his social sermons, and his remarks have all the weight of a real experience.

There can be no doubt that it is from the circumstances of his birth that Latimer derived some at least of that genuine sympathy with the condition of the country people which he enforced in such vigorous language in his sermons before Edward VI. He came from a class sufficiently prosperous to be articulate, while at the same time sufficiently near to the circumstances of the labouring people to have some comprehension of the evils which came to oppress them as the sixteenth century advanced. A man of higher birth or greater wealth could hardly have understood the peasantry and their struggles; it was a personal and intimate knowledge, which expressed itself in that homely but forcible eloquence, which was one great instrument of his influence on the nation.

Of his life at home we know little or nothing more than this. We hear nothing more of the sisters who were brought up in godliness and married with five pounds apiece. The only person connected with his childhood to whom he refers in his letters is his old nurse, Mrs. Statham, whom he frequently commends to the care and good offices of Cromwell when he was Lord President and virtual head of the Government. That he was of an affectionate and kindly disposition is evident throughout his whole life, and we may therefore fairly conclude that his relations stood in no need of his help, if indeed they survived beyond his boyhood.

He does not tell us at what school he was educated, and it is not till he came to Cambridge about 1505 that we begin to know anything about him, and even then the definite information to be found is of the scantiest. Foxe tells us that he was sent to Cambridge when he was fourteen, and we learn that he took his degree of Bachelor of Arts in 1510. Apparently he had been elected Fellow of Clare Hall in the previous year, while he was still an undergraduate. Having graduated in Arts, he proceeded, he tells us, to the study of theology and the degree of Bachelor of Divinity.

It was a time when great changes were coming over the character of learning in England. The first stirrings of the new learning had reached the country some years earlier, when Grocyn first coming home from Italy began to teach Greek in Oxford. The new ideas met with much success as well as with much opposition. Naturally enough they were suspected and disliked by those who were given to the older scholastic and Aristotelian philosophy, which by this time had hardened from its earlier condition of energetic and penetrating thought into a somewhat lifeless and traditional formalism. But from the first the new ideas, or the new learning, as the phrase went, found protection and encouragement in the very highest quarters in England.

Warham, who had become Archbishop of Canterbury in 1503, was from the first a warm patron, and he was excelled in his friendliness by Fox, Bishop of Winchester, while Cardinal Morton, the chief adviser of Henry VII., though himself not specially interested in the new learning, was a friend and patron of all men of intelligence and capacity. Under the protection of such men as these, the new ideas made considerable progress, and their influence extended rapidly at the Universities. Not many years after Grocyn, Colet, afterwards Dean of St. Paul's and founder of St. Paul's School, came back from the Continent to Oxford, fired with zeal for the study of the New Testament; and his lectures on St. Paul's Epistles marked the religious direction which the new learning was taking throughout the whole of northern Europe. All these influences were strengthened and confirmed by the visits of Erasmus to England, and yet more by his settling down in Cambridge as a lecturer and teacher.

Cambridge from this time forward was the real centre of the new tendencies. It is not easy to say why this was so. Possibly, then, as at some other times in the history of great movements, the older fashions were too strong in Oxford for the new ideas to have permanent success, possibly the removal to London of so strong a leader as Colet was too severe a loss at such a crisis; at anyrate there is no doubt that the work which had been begun by Grocyn and Colet at Oxford was carried out much more fully at

Cambridge, so much so indeed that when, a little later on, Wolsey wished to find scholars of the new learning for his college in Oxford (now Christ Church), he was compelled to import some of them from Cambridge, and it was from Cambridge that the majority of the early reformers proceeded.

We could wish that some of Latimer's correspondence during this Cambridge period had been preserved, for it could hardly have failed to throw an interesting light on the progress of the great change in educational methods which took place just at this time, and on the parallel change in the philosophical and theological opinions of educated men which began in England in the earlier half of the fifteenth century. The opposition between the old and new methods was often very intense, the old-fashioned scholars suspecting and denouncing the new as maintaining dangerous and revolutionary forms of learning, probably also as deficient in preciseness and clearness; while the new scholars found the elaborate and carefully drawn-out formulas of the scholastic philosophy dry and unprofitable beyond all bearing. They were disposed to go behind the premisses of the schoolmen and to ask whether the foundations of their system of learning were really as sure as those great writers had thought them. They refused to accept the principle of the absolute authority of any writer, whether he were a father or an ancient philosopher, and took up the position of men determined to sift and examine everything for themselves. This does not necessarily mean that they differed in all or even in the majority of serious matters from their predecessors, or that the methods of philosophical study were completely altered. It is obvious to anyone who reads our great philosophical divine, Richard Hooker, that his discussion of the nature of law, which forms the first book of the *Ecclesiastical Polity*, is founded mainly on the treatment of the same subject by St. Thomas Aquinas; and indeed, in Oxford at anyrate, the foundations of the study of philosophy always continued, as in the thirteenth century, to be laid on Aristotle. No doubt the real point of contention lay in the question whether it was better to study the New Testament and the Scriptures in general in the original tongues, or to read the enormous mass of patristic and mediæval commentary upon them; and we must admit that the older-fashioned men had something to say for themselves in maintaining that it was foolish and presumptuous to neglect the accumulated wisdom of centuries of careful and conscientious toil, and to set out to discuss new meanings in the sacred texts with a total disregard of all that had been so carefully done by learned and good men. The scholars of the new learning, however, seem in the main to tend to distinguish between the value of the writings and commentaries of the earlier Fathers of the Church and those of the scholastic writers and the theological system based upon them, and while disposed to pay much respect to St. Jerome and St. Augustine, they refused to defer to St. Thomas Aquinas or Duns Scotus.

At what time exactly Latimer came under the influence of the new learning we cannot very well decide. In all probability it was not till he had been for some years in Cambridge. Among the few notices of his life there which have been preserved to us is one in which he is represented as having at one time strongly opposed the study of the Scriptures, and exhorted the students to a more careful reading of the scholastic writers. We may perhaps infer that during the earlier years of his residence at Cambridge he was first trained in the scholastic philosophy and method of theological study, and that it was only in the latter years of his stay that he came under the new influences. What progress he made in the new studies is far from clear. In his examination before the Commissioners at Oxford in 1555, he said that he understood no Greek, but he may only have meant that in his old age he had forgotten the Greek he once knew, even as he begged to be permitted to answer in English as he had "not these twenty years much used the Latin tongue," and again prayed not to be asked to dispute, for "disputation requireth a good memory," and "my memory is clean gone." On the whole, though he is constantly referred to about 1529 as belonging to the party of the new learning, it is perhaps not wise to press this into meaning that he was at any time an accomplished scholar of the new type.

It cannot be said that Latimer's theological work, so far as it has survived, shows any indications of profound and original scholarship or thought, and indeed there are few signs in it even of any extended knowledge of the Scriptures in the original languages, and his exposition of Scripture still has a good deal of that quaintness which springs from the application of the method of mystical interpretation rather than that of severe scholarly research. The truth is, that Latimer was not without scholarship and even learning, and that his sympathies were with the new methods and results, but that the power which he undoubtedly possessed was not the power of the great religious or moral thinker, but rather that of the practical religious and moral preacher. There is nothing in any of his writings to indicate any great philosophical or theological capacity, such as is notable in Calvin, Luther, or Melancthon, or even in his fellow-reformers in England, Cranmer or Ridley. It was unfortunate, indeed, that the qualities which marked the great reformers of the Continent, the combination of profound philosophical insight with a deep religious feeling and practical capacity, were in England divided, and were found some in one man, some in another. But if Latimer is lacking in the intellectual element which did so much to promote the Reformation, which is strong in Cranmer and not lacking in Ridley, he represents on the other hand, in as fine a form as any man, the practical religious side of the Reformation, the reaction against the superstition and the formalism to which too much of religion had turned.

If Latimer's exact relations to the new learning are a little difficult to determine, it is far otherwise with his attitude to the new ideas in religion. For some years he appears to have been a confirmed upholder of the older doctrines and customs. Here we have his own account of himself: "I was as obstinate a papist as any was in England, insomuch that when I should be made Bachelor of Divinity my whole oration went against Philip Melancthon and against his opinions."[1] "I have thought in times past that

[1] *Sermons*, p. 334.

the pope, Christ's vicar, hath been Lord of all the world, as Christ is—he could do no wrong." "I have thought . . . if I had been a friar and in a cowl, I could not have been damned nor afraid of death, and by occasion of the same I have been minded many times to have been a friar, namely, when I was sore, sick, and diseased." "I have thought that divers images of saints could have holpen me. . . . It were too long to tell you what blindness I have been in, and how long it were ere I could forsake such folly, it was so corporate in me."[1] Among those who had adopted the new ideas was one Thomas Bilney, a man "ever meek and charitable," "a simple good soul, nothing fit or meet for this world."[2] This Bilney, who was afterwards burnt for holding the reformed opinions, heard Latimer lecturing to the undergraduates, and perceived that he was "zealous without knowledge, and he came to me afterward in my study, and desired me for God's sake to hear his confession. I did so, and to say the truth, by his confession I learned more than before in many years. So from that time forward I began to smell the word of God and forsook the school doctors and such fooleries."[3] We can picture the interview: the vigorous lecturer resting in his room, revolving perhaps with pleased satisfaction his address to the students; the door opens to admit the meek and simple Bilney, his heart stirred within him, seeking words wherewith to convince this man whom he admires and for whose conversion he longs, and

[1] Letter to Sir E. Baynton, *State Papers*, 1531, 607.
[2] *Ibid.*
[3] *Sermons*, 334.

finding none but a " confession " of himself. He is but a simple soul, his very simplicity goes straight to the heart of the other, and makes him see as he has never seen before. We can hardly be wrong in looking on this [1] as the true conversion of Latimer. Before this he had been active indeed in the study of the schoolmen, and remarkable besides for a certain gravity of demeanour, which had earned for him the right of carrying the University Cross, which "was only intrusted to such as in sanctimony excelled others." [2] But this talk with Bilney marked a crisis in his religious development. It was not a conversion in the sense of a turning from sin and wickedness to righteousness. He had always been earnest and upright, but from this time there was a quickening of his whole religious life, a spiritual awakening. "His fame began to grow apace . . . doing abundance of good there among the students by his sermons, which were many, by him preached both in Latin and English. The scholars flocked after him . . . before them he did prove that the Holy Scriptures ought to be read in the English tongue of all Christen people, whether they were priests or laymen. . . . None except stiff-necked went away from his sermons, which were not led with a faithful repentance of their former lives, affected with high detestation of sin, and moved unto all godliness and virtue. . . . He was also a charitable man when he was at Cambridge,

---

[1] He says he walked in darkness till he was about thirty; and again, "when I should be made Bachelor of Divinity my whole oration went against Melancthon" (*Sermons*, 334). This would seem to indicate the year 1521 as about the probable date.

[2] Strype, iii. i. 368.

according to his abilities, to poor scholars and other needy people, so conformable was his life to his doctrine. Insomuch that there was a common saying in that University, when Mr. Stafford read and Latimer preached, then was Cambridge blessed."[1] In his own account of his friendship with Bilney, he tells us that he "went with him to visit the prisoners in the Tower at Cambridge; for he was ever visiting prisoners and sick folk. So we went together and exhorted them as well as we were able to do; moving them to patience and to acknowledge their faults."[2]

We must not understand that he straightway adopted the reformed opinions as they were later held by himself. Fortunately two of his early sermons have been preserved, those on The Card,[3] preached before the University of Cambridge in 1529, and from these we can clearly enough see that his opinions at that time were not of a distinctively Protestant description. There is nothing, however, in these sermons which clearly indicates a tendency to the reformed ideas, until we come to the conclusion, where there is a strong disparagement of "voluntary works," as compared with "necessary works" and "works of mercy."

By "voluntary works," Latimer explains that he means "all manner of offering in the church, except your four offering-days, and your tithes; setting up candles, gilding and painting, building of churches, giving of ornaments, going on pilgrimages, making of highways, and such other"; which works indeed he does not condemn, but says of them that they "be of

[1] Becon, *Jewel of Joy*.   [2] *Sermons*, p. 335.
[3] *Sermons* I. and II.

themselves marvellous good, and convenient to be done." But they are not to be put beside the "necessary works," the "commandments, the four offering-days, your tithes, and such other that belong to the commandments"; or the "works of mercy," which "consist in relieving and visiting thy poor neighbours." It is perfectly clear that Latimer had no intention of breaking with the authorised church doctrine or practice, that he is only protesting against certain abuses and misconceptions in the same way as any truly pious and earnest adherent of the old views might have done. It is true that these and other sermons of the same kind raised up many opponents against him, if we may accept the evidence of Foxe; and indeed it is not difficult to understand that certain phrases were of a kind which might stir up strife, as when he explains that men who leave the necessary works, and "bestow the most part of their goods in voluntary works . . . they and all their voluntary works are like to go into everlasting damnation." Such language can hardly be described as conciliatory, and perhaps it is not to be wondered at that it annoyed and irritated certain of his hearers. But Latimer cared not. "Whatsoever he had once preached, he valiantly defended the same before the world, without fear of any mortal creature, although of never so great power and authority. . . . Vehement in rebuking all sins . . . sweet and pleasant . . . in exhorting unto virtue, he spake nothing but it left, as it were, certain pricks or stings in the hearts of the hearers, which moved them to consent to his doctrine."[1]
"Not with excellency of speech and wisdom," but

[1] Becon, *Jewel of Joy*.

out of the fulness of an honest and true heart, he spoke direct to the hearts of his hearers, and such speaking is rarely in vain.

When we come to examine critically the famous sermons on The Card, we cannot but wonder a little why they made so great a stir. They are not to be compared in simplicity and rugged force with many of the later sermons, and the conceit of the playing cards seems to us a trifle strained. There are indeed beautiful passages here and there, as, for example, when, dilating on the service Christ demands from His followers, he tells us how we shall know true love. "What!" some will say, "I am sure he loveth me well enough; he speaketh fair to my face. Yet for all that thou mayest be deceived. It proveth not true love in a man to speak fair. If he love thee with his mind and heart, he loveth thee with his eyes, with his tongue, with his feet, with his hands and his body; for all these parts of a man's body be obedient to the will and mind. He loveth thee with his eyes, that looketh cheerfully on thee when thou meetest him, and is glad to see thee prosper and do well. He loveth thee with his tongue, that speaketh well by thee behind thy back, or giveth thee good counsel. He loveth thee with his feet, that is willing to go to help thee out of trouble and business. He loveth thee with his hands, that will help thee in time of necessity by giving some alms-deeds, or with any other occupation of the hand. He loveth thee with his body, that will labour with his body, or put his body in danger to do good for thee, or to deliver thee from adversity. . . . And if thy neighbour will do according to these things, then thou mayest think that he loveth thee well; and thou in likewise oughtest to declare and open thy love unto thy neighbour in like fashion, or else you be bound, one to reconcile the other till this perfect love be engendered amongst you."[1] This surely is practical religion, and shows something of the mind of Christ. Or again: "But yet Christ will not accept our oblation (although we be in patience, and have reconciled our neighbour), if that our oblation be made of another man's substance; but it must be our own. See, therefore, that thou hast gotten thy goods according to the laws of God, and of thy Prince. For if thou gettest thy goods by polling and extortion, or by any other unlawful ways, then if thou offer a thousand pound of it, it will stand thee in no good effect; for it is not thine. . . . Another way . . . if so be that thou hast gotten never so truly thy goods according both to the laws of God and man, and hast with the same goods not relieved thy poor neighbour when thou hast seen him hungry, thirsty, and naked, He" (God) "will not take thy oblation, when thou shalt offer the same, because He will say unto thee . . . it is none of thine. I left it thee to relieve thy poor neighbour, and thou has not therein done according unto this My commandment, 'Misericordiam volo et non sacrificium.'"[2] . . . To us this reads as simple practical Christian teaching, in no way doctrinal, and saying nothing very new, only dilating and enlarging and insisting on the teaching of the Master. But in those days such preaching was not common, and, besides, there was something fresh and human about the man.

His influence grew daily, not only among the

[1] *Sermons*, p. 20. [2] *Ibid.* p. 21.

students, but with the people generally, for he preached frequently in English as well as in Latin. Morice gives us an account of how West, Bishop of Ely, "hearing of this Mr. Latymer's conversion, determined with himself to come and hear him preach, but that should be suddain and withouten any intelligence to be given to Latymer. And so it came to pass that on a time when Mr. Latymer had prepared to preach in the university a sermon *ad clerum* in Latin, the bishop, hearing thereof, came suddainly and secretly from Ely, and entered into the University Church, accompanied with certain men of worship. Latimer gave place till the bishop and his retinue were placed, and then began : ' A new auditory requireth a new theme, therefore it behoveth me . . . to entreat of the honorable estate of a bishop.'" Taking as a text, ' Christus existens Pontifex futurorum bonorum,' he so expounded it as to make the bishop feel he was not of ' that race of bishops Christ would have, but rather of the fellowship of Caiaphas and Annas.' The bishop, ' being a very wise and politique worldly man,' afterwards called to him Mr. Latymer, and said, ' I heartily thank you for your good sermon. . . . I will kneel down and kiss your feet for good admonition, if you will do one thing, preach against Martin Luther and his doctrine.' Latimer replied that he knew not Luther's doctrine, nor was he permitted to read his works, therefore it would be a vain thing to refute what he understood not. ' Sure I have but preached before you this day no man's doctrine, but only the doctrine of God out of the Scripture ; if Luther do none otherwise there needeth no confutation of his doctrine. . . . When I understand he doth teach against Scripture, I will be ready with all my heart to confound his doctrine as much as lyeth in me.' Then said West, 'I perceive that you somewhat smell of the pan, Mr. Latymer. You will repent this gear some day'; and so the bishop, never a whit amended by the sermon, practised with Mr. Latymer's foes from that day forwards to put him to silence."[1]

To us it may seem as if Latimer would have shown himself not only a wiser but a stronger man had he ignored the presence of the bishop, and quietly held on his way with the sermon he had before intended to preach. Nowadays we are inclined to think that a personal attack of this kind, from the pulpit, is not in good taste, and is calculated to do little good but rather harm to the hearer. But at least it shows that he had good courage, if he were a little unnecessarily defiant, and that he said what he had to say regardless of the effect it might have in damaging his chances of promotion, and making enemies of those who, being in a high position in the Church, had some considerable power both to injure and to advance him. The readiness of speech which enabled him to turn, as he did in this instance, from one subject to another at a moment's notice was a most important qualification for a preacher, and was no doubt one cause of his popularity.

There were, however, many in Cambridge who distrusted and disliked him. "Whole swarms of friars and doctors flocked against him on every side," says Foxe.[2] He was forbidden to preach in the university, but immediately got permission to

[1] Strype, M. iii. i. p. 369. [2] Foxe, vii. p. 451.

preach in the church of the Augustine Friars, a church which was not in the jurisdiction of the Bishop of Ely.[1] It came to the ears of Wolsey that Cambridge was troubled by two heretic preachers, Barnes and Latimer. Determined to do all in his power to extirpate heresy, Wolsey sent for these troublers of the peace, to interview them personally. He was told that Latimer was infected with Luther's heresies. He had his accusers before him, and bade them question Latimer in Duns, etc.[2] He replied, correcting their own allegations, and showing a ripe and ready learning. The Cardinal asked the reason of West's dislike. Latimer told of the sermon. "If the Bishop of Ely cannot abide such doctrine . . . you shall have my licence, and preach it unto his beard, say what he will." And herewith the Cardinal licensed Latimer to preach anywhere throughout England.

Clearly there was much stir and agitation in Cambridge. Edward Fox, Provost of King's, in a letter (1529) to the Vice-Chancellor, says that in "consequence of complaints of the shameful contentions in sermons between Mr. Latimer and certain of St. John's College, the king intends to set some order therein, not greatly to the worship of the Vice-Chancellor and other heads of the university . . . probably the St. John's men were actuated by private malice against Latimer, and animated by their master, Mr. Watson, and other friends of the Bishop of Rochester. It is reported to the king that Latimer suffers this malice because of his favour to the king's cause. Latimer, perhaps, is more vehement than becomes the evangelist of Christ, and purposely

[1] Foxe, vii. 452. [2] Strype, iii. i. 371.

speaks paradoxes to offend and slander people." Fox thinks this unwise, and urges the Vice-Chancellor to command both parties to be silent till the king's pleasure be known, or some other way is found to reduce them to concord.[1] The Vice-Chancellor seems to have followed this advice, and also to have appointed a day for Latimer to clear himself from the accusations made against him. His enemies not taking this opportunity, the Vice-Chancellor declared that any accusations made after this time would seem to be malicious.[2]

It is then abundantly evident that Latimer had in these years, between 1520 and 1530, attained to no inconsiderable eminence in Cambridge. His enemies regarded him as a hot-headed and dangerous heretic, to be silenced, if possible, by any manner of means; while his friends declared that no others preached the gospel in its purity as did Latimer; and the more impartial outsiders were clear in their opinion that he was honest and straightforward, if a trifle vehement, and should have all liberty to speak and preach at his pleasure.

[1] *State Papers*, iv. 6162. [2] *Ibid.* iv. 6176.

CHAPTER II

No incident in the history of the Reformation period in England is more difficult of treatment than the divorce of Catherine of Aragon. It is almost impossible to approach the question with any degree of impartiality. The Protestant cannot but be vexed and irritated to think that the great movement which to him stands for the struggle for religious liberty and spiritual independence should be associated, nay inextricably entangled, with so dubious and distasteful a discussion; while, on the other hand, the Roman Catholic, filled with a righteous indignation at the treatment of Catherine, can hardly be brought to see that there was any other question at issue than the matrimonial desires of the king, and impatiently, and not unnaturally, refuses to believe in the singleness of mind of any who could take part in so disgraceful a transaction as the casting off of Catherine.

As regards Henry himself, there is no trace of compunctions of heart or prickings of conscience in regard to the propriety of his marriage with his brother's widow, until he came under the influence of Anne Boleyn, and desired to be free, that he might make her his wife. It is quite possible that he may have persuaded himself that he had done wrong to marry his sister-in-law. It is hard to follow the complexities of the mind of any man, and we are all ready enough to read into our own actions, motives which an outsider would not suspect. There can be no doubt that Henry's remorse was but an afterthought, and it is not very easy to believe in its sincerity. At the same time it would not be fair to ignore the fact that others had looked on the marriage as of very questionable propriety. At the time of the negotiations for the marriage no inconsiderable dissatisfaction had been expressed, many men thinking it unlawful for a man to marry his brother's widow; and there seems to have been a general impression among the more superstitious of the people that the illness of Henry VII. and the death of his queen were sure evidences of Heaven's displeasure at so unholy a compact. We must not make too much of this, but if we bear it in mind we need not condemn as disingenuous and unscrupulous all those, and they were not a few, and among them the most outstanding of the reformers, who strove to find arguments in favour of the king's view.

Whatever his motives, then, and of a certainty his desire to marry Anne was the overmastering one, Henry was resolved on obtaining the divorce, and Wolsey soon perceived that he must do his utmost to accomplish it, if he would retain his power as a minister. He accordingly approached the pope, representing to him the danger of an outbreak of civil war should Henry die leaving behind him only a daughter whose legitimacy might well be called in question, and promising, moreover, that Henry would support the pope against Charles, and would in every respect prove himself a loyal son of the Church if the pope would but grant this, his reasonable petition. Many and severe have been the condemnations uttered against Clement for his uncertain utterances on this occasion; and there is no doubt that he showed himself extraordinarily weak and vacillating. But we must remember that his position was not a very easy one. Charles v. was at his doors, a strong and formidable foe, certain to be incensed should the pope declare against Catherine. Moreover, this marriage had been approved and sanctioned by a former pope, and Clement might well hesitate to reject the decision of his predecessor; and, on the other hand, it would be unwise and highly undesirable to make an enemy of Henry, whose headstrong self-will must already have been made evident to the pope, and who would assuredly take prompt action of an unpleasant kind should the decision be given against him. Had Clement been a man of any strength of character, had he been a pure-hearted, single-minded man, with a clear sense of what was right and wrong, just and unjust, his voice would have given forth no uncertain sound; but he was weak, and we must allow for the natural tendency of the weak man to put off any decision as long as is at all possible, in the hope that things may drift aright of themselves, that time may solve his difficulty. And Clement's difficulty was no small one, as we must confess when we consider that change of mind as regarded spiritual authority which was spreading far and wide over the Continent. It was only a pity that at such a crisis the man who claimed to be the vicegerent of Christ upon earth, and as such demanded the allegiance and submission of all Christian men, should have been of so feeble and vacillating a character.

Time passed on, and Henry saw that the decision was simply being indefinitely postponed. Even Wolsey, who as a loyal churchman had striven earnestly to keep the peace between pope and king, could not fail to understand the significance of the suggestion that Henry should go to Rome to have the case tried there. The pope was determined on delay, and would give no decision for the present. He forgot the temperament of Henry, who was all fiery impatience to see Catherine relegated to a convent or to some other dignified retreat, and to be free to make Anne Boleyn his wife. Utterly wearied of the repeated delays, and determined by some means to have his way, he began to look about him and to ask if there could be no other method of settling his business. Among those who had shown themselves especially active and energetic in the matter of the divorce were Fox, Provost of King's College, Cambridge, and Gardiner, Master of Trinity Hall, Cambridge, the one the king's almoner, the other his secretary, better known in later times as the Bishop of Winchester. "Lighting by chance in Dr. Cranmer's company at one Mr. Cressie's house, they had on design fallen upon discourse of that matter (the divorce) purposely to learn his judgment therein, knowing him an eminent noted reader of divinity in Cambridge."[1] Cranmer suggested that in his opinion the question was one to be settled by theologians, and said that he would advise the king to consult the various universities of Europe on the dispensing

[1] Strype, "Cranmer," i. 5.

power of the pope, and having got this opinion to act upon it, without waiting for the "frustatory delays" of the Ecclesiastical Courts. "If the king rightly understood his own office, neither pope nor any other potentate hath anything to do with him or any of his actions . . . within his own realm." Cranmer's words were repeated to the king by Gardiner and Fox. They came at an opportune moment. "That man hath the right sow by the ear," he said; and forthwith sending for him, he "heard him discourse upon the marriage, and well observing the gravity and modesty of the man, resolved to cherish and make much of him." He was commanded to put- his opinions into writing without delay, and to put aside all other work until this was accomplished.

We can hardly agree with Dr. Mason (in his recent work) that Cranmer was the "most guileless and unsuspicious of men," or suppose that he accepted in its literalness Henry's statement that he only sought for a dissolution of his marriage because it was a burden to his conscience. Cranmer was far too astute a man for this. We cannot praise his action in the matter; it was politic, but it savoured rather of the wisdom of the serpent than of the guilelessness of the dove. However that may be, the king took his advice, in so far that he formally asked the opinion of the great universities of Europe as to the power of the pope in such a matter. But it must not be supposed that the universities were left undirected. As far as possible they were helped to form their opinions. The University of Paris hesitated as to their verdict, and were assisted in the operation of making up their minds by a message from the French king, whose only thought was to make the rift between Henry and Charles as great as possible. All the Lutherans oddly enough were against Henry. Was it that they were honest beyond others, or only that they were far enough away from him, and near enough to Charles, to permit them to be indifferent to England? But it is unnecessary to dwell on the verdict of the continental universities; on the whole, opinion was fairly balanced.

At present our interest centres on Cambridge, for there we find on the list of those chosen to sit in Commission on the divorce the name of Hugh Latimer, and he is spoken of as favourably disposed to the king. Amongst the State Papers is a long letter from Gardiner to Henry, telling him of his visit to Cambridge and his efforts to further the king's purpose by conversation with the Vice-Chancellor and others. "On Sunday," he continues, "all the doctors, B.A.'s and M.A.'s, were assembled to the number of nearly two hundred, when we delivered the king's letter, which was read by the Vice-Chancellor."[1] At Oxford, a little time before this, the same sort of "consultation" of the university had been held. The heads of houses and the senior members generally had been disposed to be submissive and give the verdict the king desired. But the younger members were not so meek, and showed some inclination to be troublesome, whereupon the king wrote them a letter, which at once produced the desired result. Doubtless Henry thought Cambridge would follow. But Cambridge, as we have already noted, was at this time more independent in thought than Oxford, and perhaps less ready there-

[1] *State Papers*, iv. iii. 6247.

fore to submit to royal authority and grant the desired verdict. The Vice-Chancellor, having read the king's letter, "then called the doctors apart and asked their opinion . . . there was great confusion . . . and very different answers. At last they were willing that answers should be made to the questions by indifferent men, but they make exception to the Abbot of St. Benet's, Dr. Reppes, and Dr. Crome, and generally to all who approved of Cranmer's book, as having declared their opinion already. We said that way they would except all, as in so notable a question every learned man must have told his friend what he thought. . At last the Vice-Chancellor ordered every man to his seat and bade him state his mind secretly, whether they would be content with such an order as he had conceived for answer to be made by the university to the king's letter. They could not agree that night. . . . Next day the Vice-Chancellor proposed a grace after the enclosed form. At first this was refused . . . at last opponents left the house, and it was carried. . . . The grace proposed and obtained referred the question in the king's letter to the following persons, the decision of two parts of whom shall be taken as the determination of the whole university, provided the matter be disputed publicly and be read beforehand in the presence of the university:—Ten doctors, sixteen masters of theology, two procurators and the Vice-Chancellor. "We are sure of as many as are needed save three, and we have good hopes of four if we get two of these and obtain of another to be absent, it is sufficient for our purpose."[1] Latimer is one of the

[1] *State Papers*, iv. iii. 6247.

sixteen masters of theology, and against his name is the mark signifying "sure." He must therefore have expressed himself definitely on the king's side. It is interesting to note the king's peculiar method of advising with his universities, but the resultant opinion can hardly be considered very valuable. There is little further record, so far as we can find, of Latimer taking any part in the discussion of the divorce, except a somewhat lengthy paragraph in a letter to Sir E. Baynton[1] in which he sets forth the argument that "not everything whereupon followeth dissension causeth dissension." "Though it be shewed you never so often, that an opinion or manner of teaching which causeth dissension in a Christian congregation is not of God . . . I would that they that shewed you that would also shew you whether this opinion that a man may not marry his brother's wife be of God or of men; if it be of men, then, as Gamaliel said, *dissolvetur*; but if it be of God, *as I think it is*, and perchance your friends also, 'quis potest dissolvere nisi (?) qui videbitur Deo repugnare.' And yet there be many . . . who dissent from the same which could bear full evil to hear said unto them, 'Vos ex patre diabolo estis.'"[2]

In Foxe we read that a Dr. Butts, the king's physician, came to Cambridge at this time on the matter of the king's divorce. This Dr. Butts, a "singular good man and a special favourer of good

[1] Sir Edward Baynton was a relative of Cardinal Pole, the head of an ancient and honourable family in Wiltshire, and in great favour with Henry VIII. His property was within a few miles of Latimer's parish.

[2] Letter to Sir E. Baynton, *State Papers*, v. 703.

proceedings," was very highly impressed with Latimer, and it is probable enough that he reported favourably of him to the king, and that it was by his means that Latimer was brought from Cambridge to Windsor to preach before the king on the Sunday following the decision of the university. Dr. Buckmaster, Vice-Chancellor of Cambridge, in a letter to Dr. Edmunds, tells how he came to Windsor, and how he was in time to hear part of Mr. Latimer's sermon. "After evensong I delivered my letters to the king. The king greatly praised Latimer's sermon, but said, this displeaseth greatly the Vice-Chancellor yonder—yon same, he said, pointing to me, is the Vice-Chancellor of Cambridge."[1] It seems to have been very far from satisfactory to Dr. Buckmaster to have Latimer on the Divorce Committee, and we can easily understand how galling it must have been to the Vice-Chancellor to find him winning high favour with the king. Latimer must have been a constantly recurring irritation to Dr. Buckmaster at this period. He could not get quit of him. He had only been back in Cambridge a short time when he received a letter from the king (May 1530), desiring him to appoint twelve of the "best learned men in divinity" to examine, along with twelve Oxford men, certain heretical books commonly read among the people. Among the twelve selected was Hugh Latimer, who must therefore have had some little reputation in the university as a theologian as well as a preacher, although, as has already been noted, there is little trace of the learned theologian in such writings as have been preserved to us. The king in his letter

[1] *State Papers*, iv. iii. App. 1530.

to Dr. Buckmaster expresses his anxious fears as to the effect on the minds of the people of "certain erroneous and pestiferous words, sentences, and conclusions which might pervert their judgments and occasion division and contention in the chief points and articles of our faith and religion, whereon is like to ensue, unless it be repressed, the dissolution of our commonwealth." [1] The appointment of this Commission of Inquiry was speedily followed by a royal proclamation condemning "the books and disciples of Luther, and containing precepts for all law officers of the Crown and others having governance of the people to make oath on entering on office to extirpate heresy and to assist the bishops in the same." [2] A list of prohibited books was published at the end of the proclamation. The Commission were to inquire for all the English books condemned, and bring them together by a certain day. All persons retaining any such books eight days thereafter were to be held heretics and punished accordingly. The king did not apparently desire that his subjects should be deprived of the English Bible altogether, for, having conferred with the bishops regarding the inaccuracy of Tyndale's translation, he commanded them, with the help of the most learned men in the universities, to prepare a new translation, so that the people should not be ignorant in the law of God. But the bishops (according to Hall) did nothing, so the people studied Tyndale the more." [3]

It is strange to think of Latimer—and Cranmer—

---

[1] *State Papers*, iv. iii. 6367. [2] *Ibid.* iv. iii. 6402.
[3] *Ibid.* iv. iii. 6402. See note in *State Papers*.

sitting along with Gardiner on a Commission to inquire into heresies. He was very soon to show his sympathies with the heretics. The attempt at suppression had the usual result of increasing the spread of the heretical books and pamphlets. No severity could prevent men from reading the Scriptures; the Reformation movement had begun, and was not to be checked. But the laws against heresy were severe in the extreme, and much suffering ensued. The bishops had power to imprison anyone in whose possession were found any of the condemned books; they could even imprison those suspected of heretical tendencies, and there was no appeal from the judgment of the Ecclesiastical Courts. Latimer, spite of his well-known leaning to the new learning, was not among those troubled at this time. His sermon at Windsor had put him in favour with the authorities, and, though suspected, he was left in peace. But he could not look on the sufferings of others with indifference because he himself was left unassailed. At the risk of losing his newly won favour, and of damaging all hopes of future preferment, he wrote a long letter to the king, remonstrating on his action in forbidding the Scriptures to be read in English. The letter is lengthy and a trifle tedious, but it is the production of an honest, sincere man, and when considered as written by an unbeneficed clergyman to the sovereign who had it in his power to make or mar his worldly welfare, is worthy of our highest respect. He is drawn by his conscience to write to the king, feeling that otherwise he will be a traitor to the truth and to Christ. He reminds the king that, as a mortal man, he needs Christ's passion no less than his subjects, and must not disdain the lesser members of the body of Christ. Contrasting the poverty of Christ with the wealth and pride of the friars, monks, and spiritual prelates, he declares that these men are not true followers of Christ, and that they curse against and condemn others because they fear for their goods and dignities. True preachers revenge not their wrong but remit it to God, are persecuted, as were the apostles, but do not persecute. These false prelates dare not come to the light of the gospel, and therefore hinder the Scripture from being read in English. "As concerning your last proclamation, prohibiting such books, the very true cause of it, and chief counsellors . . . were they whose evil living and cloaked hypocrisy these books uttered and disclosed." As for the men who have lately been punished for these books, "no man can lay word or deed against them that should sound to the breaking of any of your grace's laws, this only except (the proclamation against the Scripture, etc.), if it be yours, and not rather theirs—(the prelates). To read the gospel does not cause insurrection. . . . Wherefore, gracious king, remember yourself, have pity upon your soul, and think that the day is even at hand when you shall give account of your office. . . ."[1] The whole letter is bold and straightforward, and, judged as the letter of a subject to his king, is remarkable for its honesty and courage. It had no effect on the king, in respect of the purpose which prompted Latimer to write, but apparently it did not displease him. With all his faults, Henry was himself bold and frank, and he could appreciate these qualities in another.

[1] Letter to King Henry VIII. (1530), Foxe, *Acts*, etc. vii. 509.

In the following year, 1531, Latimer was appointed to the living of West Kingston in Wiltshire. If we may believe Foxe, he had been appointed one of the king's chaplains, and had in consequence gone up to court, where he remained for some little time under the protection of, and in close friendship with, Dr. Butts, the king's physician. "But being weary of the court, and having the benefice of West Kingston offered to him by the king at the suit of Cromwell and Dr. Butts, he accepted that living and went to reside upon it."[1] Of this, as of much besides recounted by Foxe, we cannot however be certain; indeed, this account of his residence at court would seem to be contradicted by an entry, September 1530, in the *State Papers*, noting certain sums laid out to "Mr. Latymere" and other scholars of Cambridge for their costs to London and back.[2] If indeed he was at court at all, it must have been for a very short space. It is not clear who appointed Latimer, unless indeed it were the king. In a letter to Sir Edward Baynton he speaks of having had no "bishop's seal to show, but only a licence of the University." He speaks of the Chancellor being his ordinary, and is ill-pleased because he has to go up to see the Bishop of London, thinking that, if reform were needed, the Chancellor could reform him as well as the Bishop of London.[3] "My authority," he says, "is good enough. . . . For the University of Cambridge hath power apostolic to admit twelve yearly, of which I am one; and the king's highness . . . did decree that all admitted of

---

[1] Foxe, vii. 454.
[2] *State Papers*, v., Privy Purse Expenses, App.
[3] Letter to Sir E. Baynton, *State Papers*, v. 607.

universities should preach throughout all his realm as long as they preached well, without distraint of any man, my lord of Canterbury, my lord of Durham . . . consenting to the same." [1]

Fortunately there are some letters of this time extant, and we gather from these some idea of the manner of life led by Latimer in his country parish. "As touching the points which . . . mislike your friends, I have now little leisure to make an answer thereto, for the great business that I have in my little cure (I know not what other men have in their great cures), seeing that I am alone, without any priest to serve my cure, without any scholar to read unto me, without any book necessary to be looked upon, without learned men to come and counsel withal. . . . Sir, I have had more business in my little cure since I spoke with you, what with sick folk and what with matrimonies, than I have had since I came to it, or than I would have thought a man should have in a great cure. I wonder how men can go quietly to bed which have great cures and many, and yet peradventure are in none of them at all." [2] And again, in a letter to a Dr. Sherwood, who had accused him of rash judgment and uncharitableness, and also of preaching false doctrines, he says, " I am too much engaged in daily preaching to answer you"; and again, " I intend to make merry with my parishioners this Christmas, for all the sorrow, lest perchance I never return to them again." [3]

Here we see him absorbed in the ordinary duties

[1] Letter to Sir E. Baynton, Foxe, vii. 487.
[2] *Ibid.* vii. 491, etc.
[3] Letter, *State Papers* (1531), v. 629.

of a country parson—preaching, marrying, visiting the sick, and joining humanly and happily in the simple merry-makings of his people, struggling the while with ill-health; for he speaks of being troubled with "colic and stone," "pains in the head," and "a sickness of long standing."[1] "Nostræ gentis Anglicanæ verum apostolum," the very apostle of England, Ridley called him; no sickness or feebleness kept him from speaking the message that had been given to him; no fear of consequences prevented him from preaching boldly, both to his own people and throughout the diocese. "His fame is in most parts of the diocese," writes Richard Browne, a priest in Worcester, who has no liking for Latimer but desires to have him silenced. "He has done much hurt among the people by his preaching, he soweth errors, he said that Our Lady is a sinner, and ought not to be worshipped of the people, and divers others opinions, whereby he has sorely infect the people of Bristow. The good Catholic people there do abhor all his preaching."[2]

He was, in short, a popular preacher; what he had to say he said with a straightforward simplicity and force which could not be denied. Wherever he went he made a stir among the people, and as a consequence he made many foes. His letters are full of the trouble and annoyance from which he suffered at all hands. All manner of accusations were, as we have seen, made against him. He was charged with having said that Our Lady was a sinner, that neither she nor any other saint was to be worshipped, that he denied pilgrimages, etc. etc. He explains his position at

[1] Letter to Archbishop of Canterbury, *State Papers*, v. 859.
[2] Strype, M. i. 247, *State Papers*, vi. 246.

some length to Sir Edward Baynton, trying to make it clear just where he stands in the matter of Christian doctrine. "As for things of private devotion, mean things and voluntary things, I have reproved the abuse, the superstition of them, without condemnation of the things themselves, as it becometh preachers to do. . . . I fear me, I shall either displeasure my lord of London, which I would be very loth, or else my Lord God, which I would be more loth; not for any infidelity, but for ignorance, for I believe as a Christian man ought to believe. . . . I am ignorant in things which I trust hereafter to know, as I do now know things in which I have been ignorant heretofore."[1]

Now and again he cannot refrain from expressing his irritation with those who find fault with him. "I am not so churlish as to take amiss a Christian admonition, nor so insensible as to be always pleased at having been insulted by you more than once, and that over your cups, before I received your admonition; nay, I am not admonished after all, but rather most bitterly chided, yea assailed . . . with calumnies, and what is more, falsely condemned. . . . May God grant to me such patience, even in the midst of evil report, as becometh a Christian."[2] His words were twisted and misquoted, so that he was made to say much that was rash and uncharitable. He takes pains to refute the charges made, patiently recapitulates what he had really said in his sermons, and denies having borrowed anything from Luther or Melancthon. He stands by the teaching of the Fathers and the clear meaning of the Scriptures. Sir Edward Baynton grows troubled

[1] Letter to Sir E. Baynton, Foxe, vii. 488.
[2] Letter to Dr. Sherwood, quoted above, *State Papers*, v. 629.

about him, and writes expressing the anxiety of many of his friends,[1] some of whom think that his opinions require reformation, while others are grieved because his manner and behaviour give occasion of slander and trouble, to the hindrance of his good purposes. He trusts he will temper his judgment, and affirm no truth of himself, but have regard to the unity of the Church, and to be very sure that it is indeed the truth he preaches. Latimer writes in reply, " I am sure that I preach the truth. Ye mislike that I say, saying in reproof of the same that God knoweth certain truth. . . . As for myself I trust in God I may have senses well enough exercised to discern good and evil in those things, which without deep and profound knowledge in many things I preach not; yea, there be many things in Scripture in which I cannot certainly discern *bonum et malum*, I mean *verum et falsum*; not with all the exercise that I have in Scripture, nor yet with help of all interpreters that I have to content myself and others in all scrupulosity that may arise. But in such I am wont to wade no further into the stream than that I may either go over or else return back again, having ever respect not to the ostentation of my little wit, but to the edification of them that hear me, as far forth as I can, neither passing mine own nor yet their capacity. . . . Such manner of argumentation " (as had been used against Latimer) " may make and serve against such preachers which will define great subtleties and high matters in the pulpit which no man can be certainly sure God's word to be truth . . . as whether, if Adam had not sinned we should have stock fish out of Iceland; how many larks for a penny,

[1] *State Papers*, v. 702.

if every star in the elements were a flickering hobby; how many years a man shall lie in purgatory for one sin, if he buy not plenty of the oil that runneth over our lamps to slake the sin withal, and so forget hell, which cannot be slaked, to provide for purgatory." As for unity, what is to be said of Jerome, whose writings "caused dissension in a Christian congregation, as it appeareth by his own words . . . yet he would not cease to do good for the evil-speaking of them that were naught." With various references to the Fathers, he points out the folly of insisting on a mere formal unity in the Church. "Better it were to have a deformity in preaching, so that some would preach the truth of God . . . than to have such a uniformity that the silly people should be thereby occasioned to continue still in their lamentable ignorance, corrupt judgment, superstition, and idolatry."[1]

He is absorbed in his work as a minister, doing what he can in his parish, seeking to reform and spiritually to arouse his people, and he is worried beyond measure by these continually repeated attacks and criticisms. "Jesu, mercy, what a world is this, that I shall be put to so great labour and pains, besides great costs above my power, for preaching of a poor simple sermon. But I trow our Saviour Christ said true, 'I must needs suffer and so enter'; so perilous a thing it is to live virtuously with Christ, yea, in a Christian congregation. God make us all Christians after the right fashion."[2]

The "great costs above my power" have reference to his citation before the Bishop of London, ostensibly that he might be reproved for the "excesses he had

[1] Letter, *State Papers*, v. 703, in brief; Foxe, in full, iii. 491, etc.
[2] Same Letter.

committed" in preaching there some time previously without the special permission of the bishop; in reality because he was a person strongly suspected of heresies, and his vigorous preaching against the abuses prevalent in the Church had brought him into considerable prominence, and it may be had stirred up some little envy and ill-will against him. Latimer himself seems to have thought there were plots against him, snares set that he might fall into, and so lay himself open to reproof and punishment. Many years after, when preaching at Stamford (1550), he gave a lively account of his examinations, for they were frequent, by the bishops. "I was once in examination before five or six bishops, where I had much turmoiling. Every week thrice I came to examinations, and many snares and traps were laid to get something. Now God knoweth I was ignorant of the law; but that God gave me answer and wisdom what I should speak. It was God indeed, for else I had never escaped them. At the last I was brought forth to be examined into a chamber hanged with arras, where I was before wont to be examined, but now at this time the chamber was somewhat altered; for whereas before there was wont to be a fire in the chimney, now the fire was taken away and an arras hanged over the chimney, and the table stood near the chimney's end, so that I stood between the table and the chimney's end. There was among these bishops that examined me one with whom I have been very familiar, and took him for my great friend, an aged man, and he sat next the table end. Then among all other questions he put forth one, a very subtle and crafty one, and such one indeed as

I could not think so great danger in. And when I should make answer. 'I pray you, Master Latimer,' said he, 'speak out; I am very thick of hearing, and here be many that sit far off.' I marvelled at this that I was bidden speak out, and began to misdeem, and to give an ear to the chimney. And, sir, there I heard a pen walking in the chimney behind the cloth. They had appointed one there to write all mine answers; for they made sure work that I should not start from them; there was no starting from them. God was my good Lord and gave me answer; I could never else have escaped it. The question was this: 'Master Latimer, do you not think on your conscience that you have been suspected of heresy?' A subtle question, a very subtle question. There was no holding of peace would serve. To hold my peace would have been to grant myself faulty. To answer it was every way full of danger. But God, which alway hath given me answer, helped me, or else I could never have escaped it, and delivered me out of their hands."[1]

In one of his letters to Sir E. Baynton, he defends himself against conscious disobedience to the Bishop of London. "Forsooth, I preached in Abb-Church, not certain then whether in his diocese or no" (some of the London churches were attached to monasteries and exempt from episcopal jurisdiction), "intending nothing less than to contemn his authority, and this I did not of mine own seeing . . . but at the request of honest merchantmen, as they seemed to me, whose names I do not know . . . they required me very instantly . . . they showed not only themselves but

[1] *Sermons*, pp. 394-5.

also many other to be very desirous to hear me, pretending great hunger and thirst of the word of God and ghostly doctrine . . . I put them off and refused them twice or thrice, till at the last they brought me word that the parson and curate were not only content but also desired me." "I marvel," he goes on, "not a little that my lord Bishop of London, having so broad, wide, and large a diocese committed to his cure, and so peopled as it is, can have leisure . . . to trouble me or to trouble himself with me, so poor a wretch, a stranger to him and nothing pertaining to his cure, but as every man pertaineth to every man's cure. . . . Meseems it were more comely for my lord (if it were comely for me to say so) to be a preacher himself . . . than to be a disquieter and a troubler of preachers."[1]

In a letter to the Archbishop of Canterbury,[2] he begs to be excused coming up to London again. "Pain of my head prevents me from expostulating with you for detaining me so long from my cure. . . . The examination (before the Bishop of London) seemed endless. I am considered intractable for refusing compliance with what I deem unjust importunities. . . . I have never preached anything contrary to the truth nor contrary to the decrees of the Fathers, nor, as far as I know, contrary to the Catholic faith. . . . I have desired, I own, and do desire, a reformation in the judgment of the vulgar . . . that they should distinguish between duties . . . that all men should know that there is a very great difference between those works which God hath prepared for each of us, zealously discharging the duties of our respective

[1] Foxe, vii. 485.   [2] *State Papers* (1532), 859.

callings, to walk in, and those that are voluntary, which we undertake by our own strength and pleasure. It is lawful, I own, to make use of images, to go on pilgrimage, to pray to saints, to be mindful of souls abiding in purgatory; but these things which are voluntary are to be so moderated that God's commandments of necessary obligation which bring eternal life to those that keep them, and eternal death to those who neglect them, be not deprived of their just value." [1]

This is the very keynote of all Latimer's teaching and preaching. His heart and mind were filled with the necessity of stirring up the people to fresh spiritual life, of reforming them morally, and bringing them to a new and clear understanding of the Christian life; and with these great thoughts to absorb him, he felt the comparative insignificance of discussions about pilgrimages, the use of images, prayers for the dead—these were among the many things which, "done in a simple and honest heart, God does not condemn, yet rather . . . does in some degree approve, yet . . . would neither command nor counsel." [2] The purpose of this letter is to expostulate with the archbishop for detaining him so long from his parish, and to explain that it is impossible for him to subscribe certain articles that had been submitted to him, because, knowing the many existing abuses, he wished to do nothing by which he would help towards the continuance of superstition among the people. "Why should a preacher be called upon to recommend from the pulpit works which, though

[1] *State Papers* for résumé in English (1532), v. 854; Foxe, vii. 456.
[2] Same Letter, original in Latin.

they were seldomer performed (not to say never), I do not see that the Christian religion would suffer any loss? Let us so exert ourselves as with one accord to preach the doctrine of God, lest we become as they who corrupt and make a traffic of preaching rather than true ministers of God." These were bold words to be addressed to the Archbishop of Canterbury, by the parson of a small country parish; they are a fair example of the straightforward, plain speaking which was gaining for Latimer a reputation throughout and beyond the diocese where he laboured. The exact date of this letter is uncertain, but it belongs to the spring of 1532, probably to the beginning of March, for it refers to his refusal to sign the articles. But Latimer was not ready yet for martyrdom; possibly he thought it was hardly worth while to make a stand for such small points as those dealt with in the articles, knowing as he did his power as a preacher, and the probability that he would be permanently silenced did he continue to refuse compliance. More probably his mind was not ripe on these matters; he was tending ever to the reformed teaching, but he was not yet clear as to the essential character of some points of the doctrine.

On the 11th March 1532, Latimer, along with two other heretics, was required to sign a number of articles drawn up by the bishops, and on refusing was pronounced contumacious, and committed to prison at Lambeth. He finally consented to subscribe the 11th and 14th articles, was absolved and warned to appear again on 15th April to hear further process. It might seem that Latimer only subscribed to two of the articles; but subsequent references seem to imply that eventually he signed them all. It is interesting to note the articles, as their subscription marks a stage in Latimer's mind. 1. There is a place of purgatory. 2. Souls in purgatory are helped by masses and alms-deeds. 3. The apostles and martyrs are in heaven. 4. They pray for us. 5. They are to be honoured. 6. Pilgrimages and oblations are meritorious. 7. Vows of chastity must not be broken without dispensation of the bishop. 8. St. Peter's keys remain to his successors, the bishops, though they live evil lives, and were never given to laymen. 9. It is profitable to invocate saints. 10. Almsdeeds and other good works are meritorious. 11. Men forbidden by bishops to preach ought not to do so, until they have purged themselves and been lawfully restored. 12. Lent and fasting days should be kept. 13. God gives grace to those who receive the seven sacraments. 14. The consecrations, sanctifications, and benedictions received in the Christian Church are laudable and profitable. 15. Images are profitable. 16. It is profitable for them to be decked and trimmed and to have candles set before them.

There is a touch of sadness in a letter to Dr. Greenwood (of St. John's, Cambridge), belonging to this time. Latimer is evidently depressed and a trifle disheartened by the constant petty persecutions to which he was subjected. "As to what I have preached . . . I may at times have been a little indiscreet; yet, peradventure the misbehaviour of the people might as well be imputed to other things as to my preaching; but yet I will not be contentious. As to the people, though I will have more respect to their capacity, yet as to my old preaching I will not change the verity, and I will, with all diligence, according to my promise in my *scriptis*, do all that is in me to reprove their infirmity. There is no wretch living had more need to say with David than I: 'Reduce, Domine, a calumniis hominum ut custodiam mandata tua.'"[1]

Little or no change is perceptible in his teaching subsequent to his subscription to the articles. He continued as before to preach what he thought the truth, with the old result of large, attentive, and interested congregations, and also, as was to be expected, of renewed remonstrance and clamour on the part of those who disliked or feared his influence.

In Lent 1533, he went by the invitation of certain priests to Bristol, and preached three sermons—one in St. Nicholas' Church in the morning, another at the Black Friars in the afternoon, and the third on the Monday in St. Thomas' Church; and on these three several occasions he was reported to have taught various heretical and schismatic doctrines. The result was a serious dispute in Bristol. Various "worshipful men," notably Dr. Powell (Fellow of Oriel, afterwards Prebendary of Salisbury and Lincoln) and Hubberdine, Prior of St. James, openly preached against Latimer ("blattered against him" is his own expression); Dr. Baggard,[2] Chancellor of the diocese of Worcester, at the instigation of a Bristol priest (Rich. Brown), inhibited him from preaching, and, in short, there was such a stir and turmoil that Cromwell appointed a Commission to inquire into the disputes that had arisen.

[1] *State Papers*, v. 912.
[2] Letter from Baggard to Cromwell, *State Papers* (1533), vi. 411, App.

In a letter to Morice,[1] Latimer gives details of the circumstances of his preaching in Bristol in the Easter week, and indignantly rebuts the accusations made against him on the earlier occasion. "The priests at Bristol first welcomed and invited me, and allowed what I said. When I had gone back to my benefice, seeing that I was favoured by the people, and that the mayor appointed me to preach at Easter, they procured an inhibition against all those who had not the bishop's licence, knowing I had not, and got certain preachers to blatter against me, as Hubberdine and Powell. I brought them before the mayor to know what they laid to my charge; they said they spoke on information, howbeit no man could be brought forth that would abide by anything. So that they had place and time to belie me shamefully, but they had no place nor time to lay to my charge, when I was present and ready to make them answer."

He goes on to justify himself against misrepresentation. These preachers had accused him of saying that Our Lady was a sinner, that saints ought not to be worshipped, to have denied purgatory and hell-fire, pilgrimages, and the use of the Ave Maria. He denied all. He had indeed spoken strongly against the abuse of all these things. There were priests who spoke as if Our Lady had not been saved by Christ, and he could not let that pass. In the same way he had not derogated from the true honour of the saints, but had tried to make the people see that, great as they are, they cannot mediate for us as can our Saviour. He had indeed protested against the abuses of pilgrimage and of purgatory. . . . Provision for

[1] *State Papers*, March 1533.

purgatory hath brought thousands to hell; debts have not been paid nor restitution made; Christian people have been neglected and suffered to perish. This is surely a great and terrible abuse, and should be protested against. So too with pilgrimage. " I dwell within half a mile of the Torway, and you would wonder how they come by flocks out of the west country, to many images, but chiefly to the blood of Hales'. And they believe verily that it is the very blood that was in Christ's body . . . and that the sight of it . . . putteth them in a state of salvation. . . ." An honest servant of Christ cannot but strive his utmost to dispel these superstitions from the minds of the common people.

Meanwhile Latimer's friends were not idle, but bestirred themselves to protect him.

The Mayor of Bristol and the people generally were strongly in his favour, and Cromwell's interest had been enlisted on his behalf.[1] Dr. John Hylsey, the prior of the Dominicans in Bristol, was one of those who "opposed Latimer in his preaching," but certainly he was not of the number of his bitter foes and slanderers; for he wrote to Dr. Baggard saying that although he had felt it his duty a short time previously to do his best to have Latimer silenced, since then he had communed with him and had heard him preach, and he could not but acknowledge that "he is much more against the abuse of things" (purgatory, etc.) "than the things themselves." He even thinks it might be

---

[1] See S. Vaughan to Cromwell: "May I beg you to be solicitor to the king for Dr. Latimer. . . . It were pity to trouble or cast away a man whom many men have in so good an opinion. *State Papers*, v. 957.

well if Dr. Baggard would grant Latimer his licence to preach, "that he might open his mind in these matters that the people should be content and the council of the town be satisfied."[1]

Hubberdine was a very different kind of adversary. Latimer speaks of him as a man "of no great learning nor yet of stable wit," who "will preach whatsoever the bishops will bid him preach."[2] Possibly there may have been some truth in Latimer's reflection that the bitterness of the opposition shown him by such men as Powell and Hubberdine was prompted in part at least by self-interest: "I know the wasp that stings them. If purgatory and pilgrimage were destroyed they would lose their profits."[3] In spite, however, of the low esteem in which he held Hubberdine, he took pains to write to him at length, pointing out how grievously he had erred in speaking as he had done against the new learning, and exhorting him, as by brotherly love he was bound to do, to desist from his blasphemy against the truth.

Whether or no he was moved by brotherly love, of a certainty Latimer was stirred up by Hubberdine's attacks to a more definite defence of the new learning than any he had yet expressed. Hubberdine had accused the professors of the new learning of "living naughtily." Latimer takes no pains to confute the accusation; for "their pureness of life and virtuous living is so well known that it is but folly for me to labour" in praise thereof. Hubberdine had said that the new learning was not the truth, but Latimer pointed out that what he really objected to was no

[1] Hylsey to Baggard, *State Papers*, vi. 433.
[2] Letter to Morice, Foxe, vii. 476.   [3] *State Papers*, vi. 432.

new learning, but the old teaching of the old Scriptures. There is nothing specially remarkable in the letter, beyond the fact that Latimer speaks of himself as one of the professors of the new learning, and vigorously upholds the spread of Tyndale's translation of the Bible and various other books lately "put into" English.[1]

"From the highest to the lowest in the town of Bristol" there was agitation and excitement about Latimer's preaching; all manner of men kept writing about him to those in authority; some anxious to silence him, others to encourage him to fresh efforts. Wilson, chaplain to the king, said that when Latimer appealed he replied, "I will not take upon me to be a suitor to the bishops for you, but leave you to do such penance as ye have deserved."[2] In consequence of all this agitation a summons was sent to Latimer, bidding him appear before Convocation. Apparently he had to answer to another charge besides that of disturbing the good people of Bristol, for we find that "in the matter of certain letters to Mr. Greenwode in the University of Cambridge, he appealed to the king, who referred his cause to Convocation; whereupon Latimer admitted he erred not only in discretion but in doctrine. On his submission, he was, at the king's request, received into favour."[3] On 26th March Convocation proceeded against Latimer, touching his sermons at Bristol, having regard to his former promise and submission. Convocation seemed to think the best way to reassure the people of Bristol was to circulate throughout the diocese these articles

[1] *State Papers*, vi. 573. [2] *Ibid.* vi. 433.
[3] Froude, ii. 95.

which Latimer had signed the year before; and at the same time, Cromwell, acting now as vicar-general—a new post inaugurated by Henry as head of the Church —sent down a Commission to inquire into the truth of the various reports which had come up from Bristol. The Mayor of Bristol seems to have been much gratified by the attitude of Cromwell in the matter,[1] and it was thought that the Commission was likely to report favourably of Latimer; for we find Dr. Baggard and Hubberdine writing to Cromwell,[2] the former deprecating his displeasure for having felt it his duty to inhibit Latimer from preaching in his diocese, and even admitting that "in Rogation week Latimer preached very well, with the approbation of his hearers"; while Hubberdine insists on "the dissension and trouble" caused by Latimer and his friends, and begs Cromwell to "consider the intent of those that so grievously accused him (Hubberdine), and trusts that he will not be prejudiced by them."[3]

The report of the Commission[4] simply recounts the facts already given—how Latimer came down in Lent, preached three sermons, which some adjudged to be schismatic, and which certainly moved the whole town to controversy; how certain preachers felt impelled to controvert him, and how he had been inhibited from preaching by the Chancellor of the diocese. Otherwise the Commission did little or nothing; possibly the fact that Cranmer was now archbishop had something to do with this; anyhow, all proceedings seem to have hung fire. Evidence was

[1] Letter from Mayor to Cromwell, *State Papers* (1533), vi. 796.
[2] *State Papers*, vi. 411.   [3] *Ibid*. vi. 412.   [4] *Ibid*. vi. 799.

collected, but no action taken, unless we except the inhibition of the Bishop of London to preach within his diocese.[1] Probably Latimer was not specially anxious to preach in London, but the inhibition confirms and accentuates the remark of Chapuys, the ambassador of Charles v.,[2] who speaks of a preacher who disseminates more error than Luther, "and all the prelates save Canterbury apply to have him punished, but the king will not." Latimer is no longer a mere insignificant parish priest, but a man whose doings are remarked on by the foreign ambassadors; while the party of the new learning expect nothing from any save only from him and the new archbishop, the people favour him, and the king, though referring him to the judgment of Convocation, is yet so far his friend as to pay no heed to those who clamoured against him, and though the greater number of the bishops prayed that he might be silenced, took the trouble to recommend to Convocation that they should deal tenderly with him and restore him to favour so soon as he should submit himself to them.

Latimer had indeed one very strong friend at court in the person of Cranmer, who was now archbishop, and in high favour with the king, in consequence of his counsel in the matter of the divorce. Different as they were in character, the two men had a great mutual respect and liking; they had been thrown together a good deal, and Latimer had strongly impressed the more subtle-minded theologian by his strong and pure character. He speaks of him as "of singular learning, virtuous example of living and sincere

[1] *State Papers*, vi. 1214.   [2] *Ibid.* vi. 1249.

preaching"; [1] and there can be no doubt that the fact that Cranmer was his friend did much to neutralise the enmity of those who wished him ill.

Early in January 1534 Cranmer persuaded the king to have Latimer preach before him, thinking that he had only to be heard to be understood. He himself had been blamed for having licensed Latimer to preach, and he thought that by giving him a fair hearing before the king, he could best answer such as found fault with him, and at the same time further the truth and pure dispensation of the word of God.

Accordingly, it was arranged that Latimer should go up to London and preach there during all the Wednesdays in Lent. Modern church-goers who groan over the excessive length of a half-hour's sermon would hardly have approved of Latimer as a preacher. Cranmer felt bound to warn him [2] that he had better not be in the pulpit for more than an hour or at most an hour and a half, as otherwise he might weary the king and queen, and they might hardly continue to the end. Cranmer was clearly anxious about his protégé, and fearful lest he should not make a good impression on his royal hearers; for he wrote at considerable length, exhorting him "not to refer to matters of controversy, and to omit all speech about any special man's acts or sayings," but "to expound the Scripture according to its pure meaning."

When it was known that Latimer was to preach, [3] there was grave shaking of wise heads and much talk of the dissensions likely to arise and the trouble

[1] *State Papers*, vii. 30. [2] *Ibid.* vii. 29. [3] *Ibid.* vii. 32.

that was certain to ensue upon such an appointment. Latimer himself was no doubt well content.[1] He had for some little time wished to have the opportunity of preaching regularly before the king, " that he might himself perceive how they belie me, saying that I have neither learning nor utterance worthy thereunto."[2] He knew his own powers, and had no fear of dignitaries, and cared not at all whether or no his preaching was pleasing to men, so long as he delivered himself of the message he felt had been given to him. He spoke his mind with the utmost freedom, not shrinking from denouncing the sins of the court as well as of the people. His enemies were on the alert, and before he had preached very often it was reported that he had preached seditious doctrine. The king called on him to defend himself against this accusation, in the presence of his accuser. We have in his own words an account of the scene.[3] " Then I turned me to the king and submitted myself to his Grace, and said: ' I never thought myself worthy, nor I never sued to be a preacher before your Grace, but I was called to it, and would be willing, if you mislike me, to give place to my betters; for I grant there be a great many more worthy of the room than I am. And if it be your Grace's pleasure so to allow them for preachers, I could be content to bear their books after them. But if your Grace allow me for a preacher, I would desire your Grace to give me leave to discharge my conscience; give me leave to frame my doctrine according to mine audience. I had been a very dolt to

---

[1] *State Papers*, vi. 247.
[2] Letter to Morice, Foxe, vii. 477.
[3] *Sermons*, p. 134.

have preached so at the borders of the realm as I
preach before your Grace.'" The sedition of which he
was accused consisted in preaching against the king's
action in regard to certain of the abbeys. In his
first sermon before Edward I. he relates how he took
occasion to speak boldly to Henry on a subject
touching him nearly. The king had ordered that
certain of the abbeys should keep up his horses, and
Latimer considered that this was a misuse of the
funds which were intended for the purposes of charity
to the poor and the entertainment of strangers. " I
was once offended with the king's horses." " Abbeys
were ordained for the comfort of the poor, wherefore I said it was not decent that the king's horses
should be kept in them, as many were at that time;
the keeping of poor men thereby minished and taken
away. But afterwards a certain nobleman said to
me, 'What hast thou to do with the king's horses.'
I answered and said, 'I spake my conscience as God's
word directed me . . . God teacheth what honour is
decent for the king and for all other men according
to their vocations. . . . But to extort and take away
the right of the poor is against the honour of the
king . . . for I fully certify you, extortioners, violent
oppressors, engrossers of tenements and lands, through
whose covetousness villages decay and fall down, the
king's liege people for lack of sustenance are famished
and decayed; they be those which speak against the
honour of a king. God requireth in the king and
all magistrates a good heart to walk directly in His
ways, and in all subjects an obedience due unto a
king.'"[1] Latimer's friends were greatly troubled and in

[1] First Sermon before Edward I. (*Sermons*, 93).

sore anxiety, for Henry's hot temper was well known to his people, and it was hardly to be expected that he would calmly listen to such exceedingly plain speaking. They made no doubt the intrepid preacher would forthwith be committed to the Tower. "My sayings were well accepted of the king. . . . It is even as the Scripture saith, the Lord directed the king's heart." Henry could appreciate plain dealing. He might not be influenced so far as to change his course of action, but at least he could respect the direct speaking preacher who spoke according to his conscience and without regard to the dignity of his hearer. So far from visiting Latimer with anger, or punishing him for his boldness, he let the matter pass without further comment; and some short time after, when the bishopric of Worcester became vacant,[1] Henry appointed Latimer to the See, thus gratifying Cranmer and the men of the new learning, and sorely disappointing the enemies who had hoped to triumph over him.

For the time being Latimer's tribulations were at an end. In point of doctrine he was not yet what we should call distinctively Protestant. He held to the old beliefs in pilgrimages, purgatory, and prayers to saints, but he was keenly alive to the abuse of these doctrines and the evils that had arisen from that abuse; and the burning earnestness of his desire for reform was so well known throughout the country that he was looked on universally as one of the strongest of the leaders of the new movement, while Chapuys, writing to Charles v. speaks of his appoint-

[1] *State Papers*, ix. 151. Gostwyk sends Cromwell assent to significavit for Bishops of Worcester and Rochester.

ment to Worcester as a strong blow to the party of the old religion.[1]

It has been said that he owed his appointment to Anne Boleyn, who was taken with his simplicity and apostolic appearance; but it is more likely that Cranmer, who was his steady friend, had himself suggested his name to Henry, who knew him well enough to judge for himself as to his efficiency for the post.

[1] *State Papers*, viii. 48.

CHAPTER III

THE time of Latimer's appointment to Worcester marks a crisis in the development of the Reformation in England. Hitherto the movement had been almost entirely a political one, involving little or no change in the doctrinal position of the Church. The king was guided by his passions, rather than by a desire for a pure and reformed Church. In his anxiety to attain his own personal ends he resolved on reforms in the constitution of the Church, and as a consequence those Acts had been passed which culminated in the separation from Rome and the establishment of the king's supremacy. No doubt Cranmer and Cromwell, whose mind strongly inclined towards the Reformation, had influenced the king more decidedly than he himself recognised, leading him, and with him the nation, by insensible degrees, to graver changes than had at all been intended. Still, before 1535 or 1536 it could hardly be said that any definite religious reformation was evident in England. The sole representative of the new opinions on the episcopal bench was Cranmer, whose services in the matter of the divorce had won for him the archbishopric of Canterbury in succession to Warham. He and Cromwell worked hand in hand to promote the cause of the Reformation, but they had no help from the bishops.

Changes, however, were impending. Fisher, the Bishop of Rochester, found it impossible to persuade his conscience to submit to the Act of Succession, and fell a victim to the tyrannous decree which declared it treason to refuse to swear to the Act.[1] Worcester, too, fell vacant. Who were to be appointed to these bishoprics? The king, who was anxious to surround himself with men on whom he could rely, found that to attain that end he must select men of a very different type from those who had hitherto occupied the bench. He must in the future work on different lines, for it was perfectly evident that all the prominent men of the Reformation side, such as Latimer and Cranmer, were anxious not only for constitutional but also for doctrinal reform. This attitude of the reformers was in part the result of Henry's own actions. His determination to obtain a divorce from Catherine, and his consequent rejection of the authority of the pope, had caused him to draw near for sympathy to the Protestant princes of Germany, with the result that Cranmer, Latimer, and all the more prominent of the English reformers were infected by the spirit of the Lutheran divines. In Germany the Reformation had run on more doctrinal lines than in England, but the two countries had much in common, and above all they shared an indignation against, and a determination to be free from, all allegiance to the pope. Melancthon's letters to Henry are a proof of the close relations between the countries at one period; and though the death of

[1] *State Papers*, ix. 246, 729.

Catherine in January 1536 lessened Henry's need of this support, the two nations had been drawn into close contact, and the leaven of the Reformation had begun to work. The Church of Rome itself, which had hitherto remained unaffected by the stir of life around, could no longer resist the general movement. Paul III., by appointing pious and good men to be cardinals, began a work which in some fifteen or twenty years accomplished an immense change for the better in the great Roman Church. But a Life of Latimer is not a history of the Reformation; these things can only be noted in passing, for they cannot be properly treated; it is not possible to dwell on them at any length. It is sufficient for our purpose to notice that Henry, in filling the bishoprics of Worcester and Salisbury with men such as Latimer and Shaxton, and in surrounding himself with men of a similar type in the dioceses of Rochester, Ely, Hereford, and St. David's, was setting the Reformation on fresh lines, starting it in a new direction, with but little foresight of the goal eventually to be reached.

We have seen how in his little parish at Kingston Latimer was constantly busied with the affairs of his people, mingling in their simple festivities, comforting them in their sorrow, and in every way fulfilling the office of an earnest and faithful pastor, while at the same time he was diligent in preaching both at home and abroad, denouncing all that he saw to be wrong, and holding up before the eyes of his hearers a higher ideal of life, towards which they could not but be convinced he himself was ever striving with all the vigour of a strong nature. In like fashion, now that he was called to a larger sphere, in his appointment (1535) to the bishopric of Worcester, he occupied himself first with those duties which lay clearly to his hand. "He instructed his diocese according to the duty of a diligent and vigilant pastor, with wholesome doctrine and example of perfect conversation";[1] devoting himself at all times to teaching, exhorting, visiting, correcting, and reforming, as his ability could serve, or else the times would bear.

In the course of his visitation of his diocese his eyes were opened to the exceeding ignorance and negligence not only of the common people, but of too many of the clergy. These evils were general throughout the length and breadth of the land, and were weighing on the minds of many of the reformers. It would seem as if Cranmer, Latimer, and others had consulted together with Cromwell, for the injunctions delivered to the various dioceses are very similar in substance. A careful perusal of these as issued by Latimer (1537) throws a lurid light on the desperate ignorance and negligence which evidently prevailed but too generally.

It would seem that some among the clergy did not possess even a New Testament, for they are bidden to provide themselves with a whole Bible, or at the least a New Testament, both in Latin and English. The ignorance of the people is not so wonderful when we think of the state of the clergy, but it does seem extraordinary that a bishop should deem it necessary to enjoin that no young man or woman is to be admitted to communion until he or she have recited openly in the church the Paternoster in English.

[1] Foxe, vii. 461.

The chantry priests are bidden to instruct the children to read English, so that they may learn how to believe and to pray; they are not to discourage any lay person from reading any good book either in Latin or English, but rather to animate them to such things. The priests are every day to read over and study one chapter at least of the Bible, going through the book from the beginning to the end; in confession and making of testaments they are to stir up their parishioners from will-works to the necessary works of God, mercy and charity; they are to see to it that preaching is not set aside for any such ceremonies as processions, and to bid beads no longer than according to the king's ordinance, lest long bead-telling hinder fruitful preaching of God's word. This is no over-severe standard to set up, no impossible ideal of holiness; a very work-a-day, commonsense parson, with but little spirituality and no great intellectual gifts, could easily fulfil all that is here demanded. The "idolatry, superstition, and other enormities" resulting from the excessive ignorance and distressing negligence of the clergy, were depressing to the reformers, but they knew that progress must be slow, that only by small degrees could reformation be brought about and superstition dispelled.

Foxe has preserved for us the simple words which, as it was reported, Latimer taught the clergy of his diocese to say to the people when giving them Holy Water and Holy Bread. They are not specially impressive but they are perfectly simple, and were evidently written with the intent of impressing on the minds of the people the great thoughts which were above all else to be remembered by them, to the exclusion of all mere superstitious and mechanical notions.

In giving Holy Water—

> "Remember your promise in Baptism;
> Christ, His mercy and blood-shedding,
> By whose most holy sprinkling
> Of all your sins you have free pardoning."

In giving Holy Bread—

> "Of Christ's Body this is a token,
> Which on the Cross for our sins was broken;
> Wherefore of your sins you must be forsakers,
> If of Christ's death you will be partakers."[1]

In all ways he sought to do his duty in his diocese, and at the same time he was not neglectful to take up the cause of any who were wronged or oppressed, caring not at all that men should misunderstand and abuse him for so doing. Opinion was divided about his preaching. "Many blameth him and as many doth allow," says one of his hearers. "I heard him preach, and as my thought, very godly and well." They attacked him with ridicule, and he was called all manner of opprobrious epithets, "a knave bishop and heretic" being among the mildest; many trusted to see him burnt, one man vowing he would carry a faggot sixteen miles for that intent. A very common accusation was that he was not careful as to the men he appointed in his diocese; he might be honest, but it was most unlike, for he kept none but heretic knaves about him. "Many people think the bishop does ill to admit such a light-headed man to preach

[1] Foxe, vii. 461.

(this is in reference to the parson of Stanton); he will not suffer a D.D. or B.D. of the diocese to preach, who are known for discreet men and learned, but has admitted . . . divers light persons, to the disgust of Christian people."[1]

So far as can be discovered, Latimer was, as a matter of fact, singularly careful in his recommendations and appointments. We have a variety of letters from him to Cromwell, showing very clearly that he gave no little thought and care to this part of his work as a bishop. Cromwell had written to him recommending a certain Anthony Barker to the Collegiate Church of Stratford-on-Avon. Latimer finding that this Barker is a man of honest conversation and not without good letters, writes expressing his willingness to appoint him; "only I require two things of your lordship; the one, that the poor college be not bounden for the pension (to Dr. Bell, who had retired) . . . the other that your lordship would persuade Master Barker to tarry upon it, keep house in it, preach at it and about it, to the reformation of that blind end of the diocese. For else what are we the better for either his great literature or good conversation, if my diocese shall not taste and have experience hereof . . . the whole town is out of frame for lack of residence. When the head is far off the body is the worse."[2] Again Cromwell consults him as to the king's project of restoring the Prior of Worcester, who, according to one account, had been turned out of his office for some offence, and, according to another, had resigned voluntarily because

---

[1] *State Papers* (1536), x. 1099.
[2] *Ibid.* (1537), xii. ii. 609.

he saw ruin was inevitable. Latimer points out that the king has already shown much pity in granting the former prior a competent living, and one to wait on him, and he advises that care be taken lest in pitying of one the king "be pitiless towards many. For either he is able to discharge that great cure, and can serve God and the king sufficiently therein, or not." [1] He is quite ready to pity and help the man, but not to the extent of thereby injuring the true interests of his diocese.

Again he speaks of the bestowal of two of his benefices. One he gave to Baggard, of whom we have already heard as chancellor of the diocese.[2] He was scrupulous about accepting the benefice, and Latimer writes desiring Cromwell's advice, for he is anxious to do "inculpably and duly." The other benefice was given to Rodolph Bradford, Fellow of King's College, Cambridge, who played an earnest part in furthering the Reformation, and had been in prison for two years in Ireland.[3] When set free, he returned to Cambridge, and while there let pass no holy day without preaching a sermon. He must too have been a man of some learning as well as godliness, for he was one of those appointed to prepare the *Institution of a Christian Man*. On every occasion that we find Latimer commending men to Cromwell, he speaks temperately and reasonably, and, so far as it is possible to distinguish, the subjects of his commendation well deserve it.[4] Mr. Clopton, near Stratford, was in Latimer's judgment harsh and severe to a poor priest, Sir Large. He neither did hear him,

---

[1] *State Papers*, x. 56. [2] *Ibid.* xi. 1374. [3] *Ibid.*
[4] *Ibid.* (1537), xii. ii. 840.

nor if he had, could judge his doctrine. Latimer commends his cause to Cromwell, being himself convinced that there was malice on the part of Clopton, simplicity on that of Large. "Master Acton, his gossip and friend, has a suit to Cromwell. He is faithful and hearty in all good causes, no man more ready to serve God and the king."[1] Cromwell wishes to know of two good monks, and Latimer commends two who are with the Abbot of Westminster; "they are both Bachelors of Divinity, well learned, of right judgment, of very honest name."[2]

These instances go to indicate that, so far as in him lay, Latimer as bishop seems to have done well for his diocese. Probably it was the vigour of his speech, the force with which he denounced the evils he saw around him, that roused a certain amount of antagonism against him; but there seems to be no foundation for many of the accusations made by his enemies, certainly not for the count of surrounding himself with light men. Undoubtedly he did not love the monks, and he may have been unduly severe on certain of them, but we can hardly wonder when we read how one abbot of his diocese,[3] being bidden to London to give some account of himself, said that it had cost him seven-score pounds, and therefore required the best mitre, the best cross, and another thing or two to obtain an advance of money wherewith to pay these expenses; or how Wattwood, one of the canons of Warwick College, lingered in London enjoying himself at the College cost, caring neither for

[1] *State Papers* (1537), xii. ii. 1044.
[2] *Ibid.* (1537), xii. ii. 1043.
[3] *Ibid.* (August 1538), xiii. ii. 186.

statutes nor injunctions, reckless of the fact that the College was so poor the bishop felt bound to spare them the dues he had a right to exact.[1] An earnest bishop as Latimer was, resolved on reform, could not but be indignant at the lukewarmness of the Christianity but too prevalent among some of the monks. He himself was so determined to have his injunctions carried out that in this same College of Warwick he was himself responsible for paying the reader of Scripture, and he wrote begging Cromwell to see whether the king would not do something for the church, for " vicars and ministers sing and say unwaged." [2]

From time to time in these letters to Cromwell he makes mention of his old nurse Mrs. Statham, and begs that her suit may be remembered and furthered. It might be supposed that Latimer out of his income as a bishop could without very great difficulty have himself provided for his old nurse, but to all appearance he found it difficult to cover his needful expenditure. "I have left to myself to keep my Christmas withal, and to come up withal, three-score pounds; all the rest is spent . . . Another year and I live, it shall be better, for I thank my Lord God I am within forty pounds out of debt, which doth lighten my heart a little." The first-fruits, reparations, and other expenses incident on the accession to a bishopric seem to have been exceedingly heavy, and we must remember that Latimer did not hold his See for very long.[3] Besides, he was strongly impressed with the necessity of

[1] *State Papers* (1538), xiii. 1202.   [2] *Ibid.*
[3] *Ibid.* (1538), xiii. ii. 1133.

showing hospitality, not after a luxurious fashion, but to large numbers of people, being "more inclined to feed many grossly and necessarily, than a few delicately and voluptuously." Now he refers to his being poor, and yet charged with many expenses. "As for their school at Worcester . . . I am fain myself, as poor as I am, to retain the schoolmaster there with my livery, meat and drink upon the holiday, and some part of his living beside."[1] "The country is poor and full of penury," he says, writing to commend to Cromwell the Prior of Malvern, whom he greatly praises for his virtue of hospitality. Again we find him proposing to sue Cromwell for a piece of the demesne of Borslay, and explaining, as if afraid Cromwell should think his income ought to be sufficient, that he is treated as a ward; "no man having the name of so many things has the use of so few."

As a matter of course his labours were not confined to his own diocese.[2] As one of the most prominent men of the Reformation party, Cromwell looked to him for help and support. We find him in March 1536 acting along with Cranmer and the Bishop of Salisbury in the examination of a certain Dr. Crewkhorne, a fanatic who dreamt dreams and saw visions, and a stauncher, stronger man, Lambert, who afterwards was burnt at Smithfield. About the same time he preached a vigorous sermon at Paul's Cross, denouncing the clergy, "bishops, abbots, priors, priests, and all strong thieves." The king, he said, made a marvellous good Act of Parliament that

[1] *State Papers*, xiii. ii. 543.
[2] Cf. *State Papers* (1536), x. 462.

certain men should sow each of them two acres of hemp, "but it were all too little were it so much more to hang the thieves that be in England."[1] Bishops and abbots should not have so many servants or so many dishes, but go to their first foundation and feed the needy; they should not be "jolly fellows with golden chains and velvet gowns, ne let them come into the house of religion for repast; let them call knave bishop, knave abbot, knave prior, yet feed none of them all, nor their horses, nor their dogs. Now ye set men at liberty also to eat flesh and white meat in the Lent, so that it be done without hurting of weak consciences, and without sedition, and likewise on Fridays and all days. The Bishop of Canterbury saith that the king's grace is at a full point for friars and chantry priests, that they shall away all that, saving those that can preach. Then one said to the bishop they had good hope that they should serve forth their lifetimes, and he said, 'They should serve it out at the cart then, for any other service they should have by that.'"[2] No wonder the friars and monks hated him; little wonder if they tried to injure him by spreading ill reports of him; and, indeed, however corrupt the clergy, however depraved the monks, such language in the mouth of a preacher is surprising and requires some apology, even when we remember the roughness of the times.

Three months later Latimer again preached at Paul's Cross, this time with the purpose of "purging himself" of the false lies which had been spread against him by the enemies of the truth. It would seem, however, that the sermon did not accomplish

[1] *State Papers*, x. 462. [2] *Ibid.*

its proposed end, for the "disciples of Antichrist filled the town full, that he had openly on his knees denied all that ever he had preached." The author of this rumour, a Sir W. Blagges, parson, was discovered, and on examination he confessed that he stood so far off that he could not hear what the bishop said. While it is difficult entirely to approve the violence with which Latimer abused the priesthood, it is easy to understand that unreasonable abuse of this description must have been exceedingly irritating, and perhaps may be said to have justified the strong language of the preacher. Stevyns, who reports the occurrence, thinks the priest should be punished, as "these petty thieves are sent out by the great papistical murderers, and if he goes unpunished people will believe he spoke truth." Probably it was thought more likely that the lie would die of itself if no more notice were taken of it. So far as we can discover, Latimer took no action against his enemies either now or at any other time. We read of one man who was imprisoned for a short time, on the action of Lucy, his zealous vicegerent (a man whom Latimer held in very high esteem, saying of him, that there were few such gentlemen in the king's realm), but Latimer inquired into the matter and set him at liberty. Latimer was certainly very severe upon Wattwood of Warwick, but it is clear that he at one time paid no manner of attention to his duties, and when, after a time, he reformed and went back to Warwick "a new man," Latimer welcomed him with all possible warmth.

Yet once again in this year, 1536, he preached at

Paul's Cross, but this time he avoided subjects of dispute, "moving men to unity without any special note of any man's folly." All the lords present seemed content to give him loving thanks. Some men may wish he had stuck to such exhortations to unity rather than indulged in vituperation, but perhaps both kinds of preaching were needed.

One task set to him must, we should have thought, have been irksome and obnoxious in the last degree, yet he seems to have accepted the duty with no manner of reluctance. We refer to his preaching the sermon at the execution, or rather martyrdom, of Friar Forest of Greenwich. This Forest, Provincial of the order of the Observants, and former confessor to Queen Katharine, was found to have advised his penitents to stick to the old fashion of belief, and argued that he himself owed a double obedience, first to the king by the law of God, second to the pope by his rule and profession. By such teaching he fell under the laws of treason, but it was resolved to proceed against him for heresy. At first he abjured, but afterwards he withdrew his abjuration and declared he would not appear as a penitent. He had denied the pope, he said, in his outward but not in his inward man.[1] He was sentenced to death, and Cromwell wrote to Latimer asking him to preach the sermon at the execution.

As regards Forest's character, on the one hand, he is extolled as a model of all the virtues; while, on the other, he is spoken of as "but an indifferent person, both as respects learning and morals." However that may be, the man suffered for his convictions, and it

[1] Dixon, ii. 57.

was a hard circumstance of his fate that he should be preached at while he suffered. But it was in accordance with the ideas of the times, and Latimer clearly thought his preaching might even at the end avail to convert the poor man from his errors. He wrote to Cromwell, desiring that the stage from which he should preach might be erected so near to the spot where Forest should suffer, that not only the people might be content with the discourse, but that Forest himself might hear and be converted. And so it was eventually arranged. "A right reverend father in God, and a renowned and famous clerk, the Bishop of Worcester, called Hugh Latimer, declared to him (Forest) his errors and openly and manifestly by the Scripture of God confuted them and with many and godly exhortations moved him to repentance." It is true that in his letter to Cromwell Latimer expresses a strong desire that if Forest should yet abjure he might be pardoned even so near to the time of his execution; but the tone of the letter is undoubtedly in favour of a certain severity of treatment.

The sermon preached was of the usual kind; at the end, Latimer asked Forest if he would live or die. "I will die," he said. "Do your worst upon me. Seven years ago, you durst not for your life have preached such words as these. . . . I will be true to my faith." On this occasion the Protestant does not compare well with the Catholic. Forest, at least, met his death bravely.

Doubtless it was owing to his reputation for speaking plainly and strongly that Latimer was appointed to preach at the opening of Convocation

(June 9, 1536).[1] Most men recognised that religious matters were drawing to a crisis; the Protestant party were becoming stronger in their desire for reform, while those of the old religion were growingly anxious to heal the breach between England and Rome. Latimer was not exactly the man to pour oil on troubled waters, but at least he was bold to show the clergy their duty, and it is not unlikely that Cranmer had that boldness in mind when he arranged that Latimer should preach the opening sermon. If so, he certainly was not disappointed. Taking as his text "the children of this generation and the children of light," Latimer went straight to the subject he had at heart, the reformation of the clergy, and through them of the Church. As the lord in the parable had called his steward to give account of his stewardship, so would it be with the clergy, and what manner of account would theirs be? "Were there not some that, despising the money of the Lord as copper and not current, either coined new themselves, or else uttered abroad newly coined of other, some time either adulterating the word of God or else mingling it, some time in the stead of God's word blowing out the dreams of men. While they thus preached to the people the redemption that cometh by Christ's death to serve only them that died before His coming . . . and that now since redemption and forgiveness of sins purchased by money and devised by men is of efficacy and not redemption purchased by Christ . . . while they preached that dead images not only ought to be covered with gold, but also ought of all faithful and Christian people (yea in this scarceness and

[1] *State Papers*, xi. 123.

penury of all things) to be clad in silk garments, and those also laden with precious gems and jewels . . . whereas in the meantime we see Christ's faithful and lively images, bought with no less price than with His most precious blood (alas, alas!), to be an hungred, a-thirst, a-cold, and to lie in darkness, wrapped in all wretchedness, yea to lie there till death take away their miseries. While they preached . . . that will-works were more principal, more acceptable to God, than works of mercy . . . and that more fruit, more devotion cometh of the beholding of an image, though it be but a Paternoster while, than is gotten by reading and contemplation in Scripture, though ye read and contemplate therein seven years' space. . . . Be these the Christian and divine mysteries? . . . God would say unto us, I commanded you that with all industry and labour ye should feed my sheep; ye earnestly feed yourselves from day to day, wallowing in delights and idleness. You preach very seldom, and when ye do preach do nothing but cumber them that preach truly, as much as lieth in you . . . that it were much better such were not to preach at all than so perniciously." God would have all men read His word, "but all your care is that no layman do read it, being afraid lest they by the reading should understand it, and understanding learn to rebuke our slothfulness."[1] With a warning that God is not deceived, but sees all things clearly, and the expression of his earnest desire that he could so speak that he might seem rather to have painted a picture of the Church before their eyes, than to have spoken it, he concluded his discourse, remarkable even among his plain-spoken sermons

[1] *Sermons*, p. 33, etc.

for a directness of speech and an unsparing fault-finding. But he had not concluded what he had to say, and in the afternoon of the same day he took occasion to renew his attack on the clergy, especially denouncing their teaching of purgatory, the abuse of images, the visiting of the relics of saints, the courts of arches and bishops' consistories, "the solemn and nocturnal bacchanals, the prescript miracles" done upon certain days in the west part of the country. He did not spare his hearers, but lashed them with forceful language, which must surely have pierced the minds and hearts of some of them. The picture he paints of the clergy is a dark and dismal one, and even though exaggerated, is in itself a sufficient argument for the need of reformation; indeed, it is almost incredible that so varied an assemblage of divines should have quietly listened to his attack. He must have known very well that by so preaching he would of necessity stir up enmity against himself; it was not to be expected that Convocation would meekly submit to such an indictment as he had hurled against the Church, and many of those who were among his hearers were men of power and influence, who could hinder him not a little in his work, and might very well injure him with the king. But he was earnestly desirous, not for fresh power for himself, but for the reform of his beloved Church, and for the welfare of the people; and he felt he had here a great opportunity which must be seized whatever the consequences to himself.

Besides being noteworthy because of this picture of the corruptions of the Church, this sermon is of great interest as showing the progress of Latimer's mind in regard to various of the Reformation doctrines. When he was accused some three years before by Hubberdine and others of having preached that there is no purgatory after this life, he strongly denied having said any such thing. Even at that time, it is true, he was careful to point out the evil that resulted from the insistence on purgatory, declaring that it was a vain thing to neglect present and evident duty to our neighbours on earth in order to benefit the souls of the dead; for neither the "singings nor sayings of priests will help us out of hell, if, while on earth, we forget God's commands to love our neighbour." But in the sermon to Convocation he goes much further,[1] inveighing against purgatory, as "our old ancient purgatory pick-purse, that was swaged and cooled with a Franciscan's cowl, put upon a dead man's back, to the fourth part of his sins . . . the wise fathers and genitors of this purgatory were the wisest of all their generation. . . . It was a pleasant fiction and so profitable to the feigners of it that almost, I dare boldly say, there hath been no emperor that hath gotten more by taxes and tollages of them that were alive, than these the very and right begotten sons of the world got by dead men's tributes and gifts." So, too, in the matter of images, he earnestly begs Convocation to take action about them, pointing out how the people were deluded by St. Blesis' heart at Malvern, and St. Algar's bones, and other "juggling deceits"; how, too, often pilgrimages were taken to "visit pigs' bones, instead of saints' relics," and the "miserable people were still suffered to take the false miracles for the true and to lie still asleep in ignorance." Possibly

[1] *Sermons*, p. 50.

his increased knowledge of the state of England, gained by his episcopal experience, had emphasised to his mind the pressing need of reform, and opened his eyes to the true character of certain doctrines which until now he had held in all sincerity, thinking the evil so often resulting from them not integral to their character, but due only to their abuse.

Not much was accomplished by this meeting of Convocation. The two parties were somewhat bitter against each other; those of the old learning making a long list of heretical opinions, and drawing up a bill condemning them; the Protestants debating and discussing with no little virulence. After some days' fruitless discussion, Cromwell, as Vicar-general, came and bade them, in the king's name, come to an end. Little was done, but indeed little could be done. Reform must be gradual, and the people must be taught by slow degrees. Latimer was not prominent in debate. Burnet speaks with some contempt of him as a public character, but indeed his desire was not to shine in Convocation, but rather to do his duty in his diocese. It is not unlikely that he helped Cranmer to draw up certain articles against relics, images, and pilgrimages; but his talents were not those of a statesman, and it is noticeable that there is little reference to him with regard to the more important matter of administration. The time was such that it was difficult for a man of his somewhat uncompromising bluntness to take much useful part in formal discussions, both his virtues and his failings were of a kind that made him unfit for this. He was not inclined to be reticent with regard to his own opinions, nor had he, so far as we can judge, any great power of self-restraint in expressing himself with regard to those from whom he differed.

There was still one great change to be carried out by Parliament at the period of the Reformation, — the suppression of the monasteries. In 1535 the king had ordered a general visitation of the monasteries throughout England. The report brought back by the visitors was melancholy and depressing, beyond all expression. The chief members of many of the religious houses were accused of leading loose lives, and generally of irregularities not to be tolerated in laymen, far less in those who professed a peculiar sanctity. We must, however, be careful not to accept these reports without question. Recent investigation, especially that of Father Gasquet, has thrown fresh light on the monastic life, and it must be confessed that there was great, if not gross, exaggeration in the report presented by Parliament. No doubt there was much that was evil, and above all great laxity and self-indulgence, and it is not at all unlikely that Cranmer was right in thinking that the monasteries, taken altogether, were so far from a help to the progress of the Reformation that they hindered and kept back the movement. But it is not possible to approach the subject impartially without perceiving clearly that the visitors were not unbiassed, and there can be no manner of doubt as to the king's object and desire. Henry knew that the monks were opposed to him, in the matter of the divorce among other questions; and while he desired reform, and may honestly enough have been scandalised by the reports of much that went on in the convents, his main object was to enrich himself and his favourites with the great revenues belonging to many of the religious foundations. The reformers themselves were greatly divided in opinion as to what should happen to the monasteries. All desired reform, but very few contemplated suppression. Cranmer, indeed, was strongly persuaded that the existence of the monasteries was impossible if the religious life of the country was to be really reformed; but even he seems to have perceived the difficulty of secularising the property; his idea apparently was to found a number of bishoprics out of the revenues, thinking that if the dioceses were smaller the bishops might better control them. Latimer and with him many of the reformers were strongly, even bitterly, opposed to the secularising of any property which had been specially given to God. At first, indeed, Latimer could not even see his way to monks leaving their profession: "I myself have racked Scripture . . . and have expounded it against religious persons that would forsake their order which they had professed and would go out of their cloister."[1] Instead of taking the lands from the abbeys, he would have made every effort to reform the ecclesiastical bodies; and supposing these proved to have too much wealth to be compatible with spiritual life, he would have had their wealth transferred to the high and true interests of religion, such as the education of the young. He entreated Cromwell[2] to take measures to prevent the suppression of the Priory of Great Malvern, praying him that it might be left "not in monkre, but any other ways as would seem good to

[1] *Sermons*, p. 60.
[2] *State Papers*, xiii. ii. 1036.

the king's majesty, as to maintain learning, preaching, study, with praying and good housekeeping." He was too shrewd to have any doubts as to the king's real motives, and could fairly judge what value was to be set on the indignation he professed against the wicked lives of the monks. In a sermon preached before Edward VI. Latimer says: "I would not that ye should do with chantry priests as ye did with the abbots, when the abbeys were put down. For when their enormities were first read in the Parliament House, they were so great and abominable that there was nothing but 'down with them.' But within a while after, the same abbots were made bishops . . . to save and redeem their pensions. 'O Lord! think ye that God is a fool and seeth it not.'"[1] In another sermon of the same time he grieves over the diverting of abbey property, and wonders greatly, when he considers "what hath been plucked from abbeys, colleges, and chantries that no more has been bestowed on this holy office of salvation. . . . Schools are not maintained, scholars have not exhibitions, the preaching office decayeth. Men provide lands and riches for their children, but this most necessary office they for the most part neglect. Very few there be that help poor scholars . . . I wish ye would bestow as much upon this necessary office of salvation, as in times past ye bestowed on pilgrimages, images, and such vain things of the Romish Pharisees' and papists' inventing."[2] Henry, indeed, saw in the monasteries a new mine of wealth. He was in need of money, and the abbeys were rich. Cromwell knew very well that many, nay most of the reforming clergy, could not approve of

[1] *Sermons*, p. 123.   [2] Sermon at Stamford, 1550.

any such high-handed action as the appropriation of Church funds for secular purposes; but he cared not at all. He had to provide the king with money, and here was wealth in abundance. It is very probable that he was also anxious for reform, but it is hardly to be believed that the desire for reform was the prevailing motive either with him or with the king. After some discussion, an Act was passed altogether suppressing the lesser monastic establishments, their property passing to the Crown, and the monks being transferred to other monasteries or pensioned off, or, as Latimer remarked, made bishops to save the pensions.

These great changes could not be carried through without exciting great opposition, for it is clear that Henry VIII. had to use the strongest pressure to induce Convocation and Parliament to assent to the various measures laid before them. The discontent came to a head at last in the great Northern Rebellion, generally called the Pilgrimage of Grace, in 1536. Discontent was not by any means confined to the priesthood. The power of the Church was stronger in the Northern counties than in the South. The Northern character, more rugged and fierce, is possibly more dogged and obstinate in its attachment to old superstitions, as well as more loyal and faithful to old friends. For one reason and another the people were attached to the old forms and customs, and their indignation against those who came to suppress the monasteries was intense and outspoken. Indeed, the methods in which reform was carried out were far from conciliatory. Rumour was rife with tales of the outrageous behaviour of the visitors' followers, of the church plate being manufactured into dagger hilts, of bold coarse men riding the country dressed in the priests' vestments. Naturally such action roused bitter resentment, and that not merely in the minds of the priests but also of the nobles and common people. These had wrongs of their own, which burned within them. The great nobles hated Cromwell with a bitter hatred because of his ignoble origin and his policy, which was steadily opposed to their interests. It had been bad enough to be governed by Wolsey, but at least he was a Churchman, and Cromwell had not even that claim to their loyalty. He was rough and downright, and, worst of all, he was successful in spite of bitter opposition. Moreover, he did not confine his reforms to the clergy. A strong man, he saw confusion and corruption on every hand, and hesitated not at all to stretch out the hand of reform touching an evil here and there. The nobles had their private grievances against him, and the poor people were filled with discontent, for they were now beginning to suffer from the changes in agriculture, etc., and all their troubles they not unnaturally attributed to those who were in authority. All these causes were at work in the outbreak in the North, the Pilgrimage of Grace as the insurrection was called; but the chief cause of trouble was undoubtedly the suppression of the monasteries and the proposed reform of the Church. An account of the rising was sent to Lord Chancellor Audeley by some one calling himself a gentleman of Holland in Lincolnshire.[1] He and others have tried to persuade the people

[1] *State Papers* (1536), xi. 585.

of the danger of such a rebellion, but in vain. They could not die in a better quarrel than God's and the king's. They are resolved on certain reforms, that the Church of England shall have its accustomed privilege, "without any exaction," that suppressed monasteries shall be restored, "except such as the king hath suppressed for his pleasure only" (a curious exception), and that they shall have delivered up to them, or banished the realm, my Lord Privy Seal and the heretic bishops. The insurrection is the most dangerous that hath been seen, and all rises from persons of no reputation. In the articles submitted by the rebels to the king they express their grief that there are bishops of the king's late promotion who have subverted the faith of Christ, and among those specially mentioned is the Bishop of Worcester.

The rebellion was but shortlived, being put down with a strong hand and merciless severity. The evidence of various of the leaders when on trial showed the general feeling of the people, and to a great extent explained their soreness and discontent. John Halom, yeoman, one of the leaders of the rebellion, when examined,[1] alleged as causes for the rising—(1) The king's visitors coming to Lowthe to take away the relics and spoil the church; (2) the plucking down of abbeys; (3) the payment of the quintain firstfruits and tenths; (4) new laws in the Church, and other things, such as that there should be but one parish church in four miles, but one chalice in a church, and that all church stocks or crosses, copes, all but one,

[1] *State Papers*, xii. i. 201.

and other ornaments of churches should be taken away. "*Because people saw* many abbeys pulled down, they believed the rest. Every man cried against Cromwell, Cranmer, and Latimer." Aske, the most interesting of the leaders, trusted to see these bishops have an evil end for filling the realm with heresy. He and all the commons favoured insurrection, because they would have the said bishops (Canterbury, Worcester, Rochester, and St. David's) deprived, supposing them to be the occasion of the breach of the unity of the Church. They were reputed to be of the new learning, and maintainers of Luther's and Tyndale's opinions. It was owing to them that religion was not favoured. As for himself, Aske, he knew not the difference between heretic and schismatic, but they varied from the old usages and ceremonies of the Church, and so they were bruited schismatics.

Pickering, another of the rebels, "meant by heretics the bishops of Canterbury, Worcester, and Salisbury, and by tyranny, the violent setting forth of their heresies."[1] There is a certain simplicity about these confessions, a unanimity not unknown in later days; what is orthodox may not be certain, but these men are heretics, and what they teach is heresy.

The rebels were especially bitter against the Bishop of Worcester. The report that he had recanted had spread to Lincolnshire and seemed to add to their bitterness. Many wished they could see him die. The truth is no doubt that not only was Latimer one of the most prominent men on the reformed side, but his Protestantism became more decided from day to

[1] *State Papers*, xiii. 1021.

day. He was growingly convinced of the evil resulting from the ignorant and superstitious worship of images and relics. In 1538 he was commissioned by the king to go to the abbey of Hales,[1] in Gloucestershire, to examine the famous relic known as the "blood of Hales," and supposed to be a portion of our Saviour's blood, the object of endless pilgrimages and devout worship. He writes to Cromwell, giving a full and particular account of the blood as he found it on examination. It was "enclosed in a round berall, garnished and bound on every side with silver, which we caused to be opened in the presence of a great multitude," and taken out of the berall. "In the glasse it looks a glistering red, but a little being taken out it was found to be yellow like amber or casse gold. It was wondrously closely and craftily enclosed and stopped up, and cleaves fast to the foot of the little glass. It seems to be an unctuous gum and compound of many things. It has an unctuous moistness, and though it seems like blood in the glass, when taken out it turns yellow and is cleaving like glue—or bird-lime."[2] Having examined it carefully, and to their own satisfaction clearly proved the imposture, he and those acting with him enclosed it in red wax sealed with seals and locked it in the coffer of the abbey until the king's pleasure should be known.

It was thought by the king that the exposure of the frauds of which the monks had too often been

---

[1] It was the "bluddy abbot" of Hales, in whose custody this precious relic was kept, who required the best mitre and cross to provide for his visit to London. See above, p. 66.

[2] *State Papers*, xiii. 709.

guilty would do much to rouse the indignation of the people against them, and as a consequence to justify the king's action in suppressing so many of the religious houses. By command of the bishops, a great collection of wonder-working relics was conveyed on horseback to London; a sermon was preached at St. Paul's, and an image called the Rood of Grace in Kent was first exhibited to the people; then the fraud concerning it being explained, the image was broken to pieces and committed to the flames. Then Latimer, in the western end of the cathedral, held in his hand a small image which the country people had said eight oxen could not move, and flung it out of the church.

In a letter to Cromwell, Latimer expresses a strong desire that he will bestow the great Sibyl of Worcester to some good purpose, "ut pereat memoria cum sonitu." This was the image of Our Lady at Worcester, which, when stripped, proved to be the statue of some bishop.[1] Latimer writes: "She hath been the devil's instrument to bring many (I fear) to eternal fire; now she herself, with her old sister of Walsingham, her young sister of Ipswich, with their other two sisters of Doncaster and Penrice, would make a jolly muster in Smithfield; they would not be all day in burning." It was an innocent enough desire, and seems to have been, to some extent, carried out: the sight surely was a better one than the burning of Forest, and probably more profitable to the cause of the Reformation.

The king had found it necessary to authorise the printing of an English Bible. In 1526 Tyndale

[1] *Remains*, 395, note.

completed the New Testament, and this had been rapidly distributed throughout England. It was soon followed by a translation of the whole Bible. The bishops strongly disapproved of this work, whereupon the king advised them to set to work themselves and produce a better translation.[1] After considerable delay a translation was produced, based upon Tyndale's, but with certain changes, and this was in 1536 ordered to be placed in the churches.

Having seen to it that his people should hear the Scriptures read regularly in the common tongue, Henry thought his next step must be to explain in some detail the true doctrine of the Church. He had frequently explained that he had not in any way departed from his true loyalty to the Church. All he had done was to cast off the usurped authority of Rome. But in the minds of the people there was much confusion, and the king felt it incumbent on him to clear up that confusion. With this pious intent, he caused to be drawn up and published Ten Articles devised by the king's highness majesty, to stablish Christian quietness and unity among us, and to avoid contentious opinions. Acceptance of the Scriptures and the three creeds—baptism, the sacrament of penance, the presence of Christ's body and blood in the Eucharist, briefly stated, Justification,—these are the points dwelt on in the first part of the articles, and these are described as "commanded expressly by God, and necessary to our salvation." While the second part "containeth such things as have been of a long continuance for a decent order and honest policy, prudently instituted and used in

[1] *State Papers* (1530), iv. 6402, note.

the churches of our realm, although they be not expressly commanded of God nor necessary to our salvation,"[1]—these are, the use and abuse of images, the honour of the saints, the meaning of certain rites and ceremonies, and of purgatory, that "the place where the dead be, the name thereof and the kind of pains be to us uncertain by Scripture."

These articles propounded to "be approved by the consent and determination of the whole clergy of this realm"; but so far was this from being true that in the North the clergy met and passed resolutions against them, and throughout the country the general dissatisfaction with the king and his measures expressed itself in various ways. But Henry was pleased with his success so far as it had gone, and in the beginning of 1537 Cromwell, as his representative, called together the bishops and desired them to form a committee to draw up a fuller exposition of the doctrine of the Church.

"There be weighty controversies now moved and put forth not of ceremonies and light things, but of the true understanding, and of the right difference of the law and the gospel; of the manner and way how sins be forgiven; of comforting doubtful and wavering consciences . . . of the true use of the sacraments . . . which be the good works and the true service and honour which pleaseth God. . . ."[2] These were some among the items set before the consideration of the clergy by Cromwell. A committee was formed, composed of men so divergent in opinion as Cranmer and Bonner, Latimer and Gardiner, Stokesley and

---

[1] From Mason's *Cranmer*, p. 98.
[2] *Ibid.* p. 100.

Shaxton, and the result was the publication of the *Institution of a Christian Man*, popularly known as the Bishops' Book. It contained an explanation of the Creed, the Seven Sacraments, the Commandments, the Paternoster, and the Ave Maria, Justification and Purgatory.

The Bishops' Book, in matter of doctrine, is in much the same position as the Ten Articles, and indeed on various points, such as penance, purgatory, and the Eucharist, it simply repeats the articles with some slight verbal changes. The sacraments, seven in number, are of differing importance; baptism, the Holy Supper, and penance being reckoned to be of a higher order than the rest, they having been instituted by our Lord Himself. The Ave Maria is not a prayer but a song of praise; the Church of Rome has no claim to paramount rule, but is only one of the Churches of Christ. There is a long chapter on the Sacrament of Orders. This is declared to have been "instituted by Christ and His apostles in the New Testament"; it has for visible sign "prayer and imposition of the bishops' hands," and has "annexed unto it assured promises of excellent and inestimable things." The Word and the Sacraments are the "ordinary mean whereby God will make us partakers of the reconciliation which is by Christ," and for the dispensing of the Sacraments a ministry is necessary. It is interesting to compare this statement with Cranmer's expression of his own opinion on the subject, as contained in his answers to the questions sent round to all the bishops in 1540, with a view to the compilation of the King's Book, which in 1542 superseded the Bishops' Book. "All

Christian princes," he says, "have committed unto them immediately of God the whole cure of all their subjects, as well concerning the administration of God's word for the cure of souls as concerning the ministration of things political and civil governance, and in both these ministrations they must have sundry ministers under them. The civil ministers under His Majesty . . . be the Lord Chancellor, Lord Treasurer, etc. The ministers of God's word under His Majesty be the bishops, parsons, vicars," etc. . . . " In the admission of many of these officers be divers comely ceremonies and solemnities used, which be not of necessity, but only for a good and seemly fashion; *for if such offices and ministrations were committed without such solemnity, they were nevertheless truly committed.* And there is no more promise of God that grace is given in the committing of the ecclesiastical offices than it is in the committing of the civil office." " In the apostles' time," he goes on, " because there were no Christian princes to govern the Church, ministers could only be appointed by the consent of the Christian multitude among themselves. They took such curates and priests as they knew to be meet, or as were commended to them by men replete with the Spirit. Sometimes the Apostles appointed them, in which case the people with thanks accepted them, not for the supremity, impery, or dominion that the Apostles had over them to command, as their princes and masters, *but as good people*, ready to obey the advice of good counsellors. . . . A bishop may make a priest by the Scripture, and so may princes and governors also, and that by *the authority of God committed to them* and the people also by their election; for as we read that bishops have done it, so Christian emperors and princes usually have done it, and the people, before Christian princes were, commonly did elect their bishops and priests."[1]

Cranmer had undoubtedly a strong voice in the committee engaged in the compiling of this book, but it is not unlikely that he found his colleagues by no means pliable or easy to work with. The committee was composed of very varying elements, and it is not surprising that they found some difficulty in fusing. Latimer, writing to Cromwell, to tell him the much-discussed book approaches completion, and will be sent to him shortly, says he would rather be the poor parson of Kingston again than continue thus Bishop of Worcester. "Forsooth, it is a troublous thing to agree upon a doctrine in things of such controversy, with judgments of such diversity, every man (I trust) meaning well, and yet not all meaning one way. But I doubt not in the end we shall agree both one with another, and all with the truth, though some will then marvel."[2] He prays that it will be well and sufficiently done, so that there will be no need to have any more such doings. It seems as if we can trace Latimer's hand in the chapter on purgatory: "the place where they (the departed) be, the name thereof and kind of pains there be to us uncertain by Scripture, so that the abuses connected with the doctrine ought to clearly put away, such as that the Bishop of Rome's pardons or masses said at Scala Coeli, or otherwhere, could send souls straight

[1] Mason, *Cranmer*, pp. 102, 103.
[2] *State Papers* (1537), xii. ii. 295.

to heaven."[1] In a long and elaborate paper on Purgatory, evidently written during the compilation of the Bishops' Book,[2] he gathers together a number of passages from the Fathers, Augustine, Jerome, Hilary, Cyprian, and Chrysostom, and shows that among them there was great diversity of opinion in regard to purgatory. It is best then to take the teaching of Scripture; for, indeed, when we come to examine carefully the teaching of the Fathers, or the popular views current among us, we shall find that it is more easy to accept than to reject all that they say which is not also said in the Scriptures; and Scripture does not definitely say that there is a purgatory. He concludes by saying that the founding of monasteries argueth purgatory to be, so the putting of them down argueth it not to be. What uncharitableness and cruelness seemeth it to be to destroy monasteries of purgatory. Now it seemeth not convenient the Act of Parliament to preach one thing and the pulpit another clean contrary. Side by side with Latimer's arguments against purgatory and his quotations from the Fathers can be seen the comments of the king—comments showing no little shrewdness and common sense, and even a superiority to Latimer in force of argument.

To return, however, to the Bishops' Book. It can hardly be said to mark very definitely the position of the Reformed Church, but may be taken as a fair representation of the views of such men as Cranmer and Latimer, though modified to some extent by the opinions of the less advanced members of the com-

[1] Mason, *Cranmer*, p. 99.
[2] *State Papers* (1537), xii. i. 1312.

LIFE OF LATIMER

mittee. It is a rather remarkable document, when we consider the diversity of opinion among those who compiled it; but it cannot be said to have had the sanction of the Church as a whole, and the king himself refused to authorise it. In the country at large there was no little confusion of mind. Among the *State Papers* there is a letter from a certain Mr. Butler, giving an account of the general state of affairs. " Here ceremonies are still tolerated, but explanations are added, as that holy water is but to remind us of the sprinkling of the blood of Christ; the bread signifies the breaking of His body, etc. Nothing is as yet settled as to the marriage of the clergy, though some have freely preached before the king on the subject. The mass is not called a sacrifice, but a representation of Christ's Passion. All images that are worshipped are removed. The chief supporters of papacy among us are cut off—the Marquis of Exeter, Montague, Earl of Salisbury, Sir E. Nevill. It is said we are to have war with French, Italians, Spaniards, and Scots at once. The pope has procured the burning of three English merchants in Spain, and granted remission of sins to whoever shall kill an English heretic. We are all as yet unmarried. The Archbishop of Canterbury is busy teaching the people, and composing discourses in English to be used by the clergy instead of Latin."[1]

Cranmer would seem to have been well content with the progress of events. The Scriptures were translated into English, and were read in the parish churches; the doctrine of the Church had been

[1] *State Papers* (1539), xiv. i. 466.

published, so that men might instruct themselves therein; the king, as he thought, was full of a pious zeal for the reform of the Church, and for the establishing of real religion among his people. Cranmer thought he ought therefore to busy himself in his diocese, and proceeded to carry out a very thorough visitation, inquiring how the people were affected towards the king, and how far they carried out the injunctions which he and others of the bishops had, at the instigation of the viceregent, issued some time before.

Latimer likewise occupied himself with the cares of his diocese, much relieved to have finished the harassing task of the Book of Doctrine. The result of the visitations could hardly be described as encouraging. The old superstitions could not be rooted out of a sudden. Many of the clergy were in strong opposition to the new movement, and preached slightingly concerning the king's supremacy, or boldly confessed their loyalty to the pope, and found many who heard them gladly. More especially were they opposed to the diminution of holy days. These had been so very numerous as seriously to interfere with the despatch of business, and even with the inbringing of the harvest; and they were too often the occasion for rioting and debauchery, besides being instrumental in encouraging the superstitious idolatry of images.

It was necessary to diminish their numbers, but it is highly probable that the reformers erred in making too great and sudden changes. People had been for long accustomed to keep the feast of Thomas à Becket, for example, and it might have been more wise to gently discourage rather than wholly to forbid the celebration of a feast so general and of so considerable a tradition. But the fiat went forth from Parliament, and all feasts, save only those of the Twelve Apostles, of Our Lady, St. Michael, and Mary Magdalene, were henceforth forbidden; no bells were to be rung, no churches adorned, no processions to take place in honour of any other of the saints. It is not hard to understand that such an edict would rouse some opposition, and even resentment, among the people, many of whom would only perceive that their task-days were increased and their pleasure-days lessened, without any sufficient reason. And there were many priests who would foster such ideas, many like the parson of Wincanton, who warned his people against "these new-fangled fellows who read these new books, for they be heretics and knaves and Pharisees," and are "like to a dog that gnaweth on a mary bone and never cometh to the pith."[1] If any man praised the New Testament, this curate was ready to fight him, and it was said of him that he "applieth in such wise his school of fence so sore continually that he feareth all his parishioners therewith." He was given to dicing, carding, bowling, and such other edifying games, and bore a special hatred to Latimer, trusting that he might see him burned "with all the new books in England about him." The bishops had no easy task before them in contending against men of this description, and they cannot be blamed for taking summary means of discipline and punishment. Little could be done without the consent of the vicegerent, Cromwell, to judge at least from Latimer's letters, and the extra-

[1] *State Papers* (1539), xiv. i. 897.

ordinary number of details with which he troubles his superior. He commits the cause of this man and that to his "singular good lord"; sends Butler of Droitwich to certify to him the misbehaviour of a certain priest; begs Cromwell to interfere in the suit of Mr. Nevill, as his marriage depended on it; prays that he will no longer suffer William Clapton to rage, for otherwise it will be but folly for any true preachers to come into that part of Latimer's diocese; and, in short, as he himself says in one of these letters, refers all things to Cromwell's "approved wisdom." Again, he says: "Sir, I know that I am a bold fool, but till you rebuke me for the same, I must needs be malapert with you for such honest men." And again: "I ascertain you before God that I never presented any matter unto you of any malice or ill-will to any person, but only of good zeal to the truth and discharging of my duty." And indeed, this seems to be a true statement. Latimer's clients would appear to have been not only in need of assistance, but so far worthy of it, as that they were generally honest and occasionally learned. He "likes not honey-mouthed men, whose deeds and acts are not according to their words." Honesty is the quality he most diligently seeks for, and seeks to commend to his friend; for Cromwell surely was a friend to Latimer, and was held by him in high esteem and affection. "God prosper you," he writes. "You, one man, have promoted more honest men, since God promoted you, than hath many men done before your time, though in like authority with you"; and again: "God send you well again to us (he was ill with the ague), for without you we shall make no end"; and again: "You be indeed *sciens artifex*, and hath a good hand to renew old bottles, and to make them apt to receive new wine."[1] The correspondence between them was full and frequent, and has no appearance of restraint, but rather of frank friendliness.

About the time of the completion of the Bishops' Book, Latimer had occasion to be in London, to preach in accordance with the curious instructions of the will of one Humphrey Monmouth, who had died but a little while previously.[2] This man had been a considerable draper, and an alderman of some little importance in London, pre-eminent among others not only by his wealth but by a very uncommon piety. Among the earlier patrons of the Gospellers he did much to further the printing of the Scriptures, and in the year 1528 was committed to the Tower on the charge of heresy, it being declared that he bought and read Luther's Works, helped Tyndale, and, generally speaking, held the new learning. He petitioned Wolsey and the Council, and was set free, but assigned to the care of Tunstal, Bishop of London. Not deterred by his imprisonment, he continued to frequent the sermons of the reformers, more especially of Latimer, for whom he conceived a great admiration. By his will[3] in 1537 he forbade any branches or hearse to be used at his funeral; no dirge was to be sung or said, only four or six stiff torches were to be burnt. Immediately after the funeral a sermon was to be preached by Dr. Barnes, Dr. Crome, or Dr. Taylor, to the glory of God and the witness of Monmouth's

[1] *State Papers*, xiv. i. 740.   [2] Strype, i. ii. 487.
[3] *State Papers*, xii. ii. 1100.

faith. The Bishop of Worcester and these three clergymen were to preach in the testator's parish church two sermons weekly till they among them have preached thirty sermons, for each of which they are to get 13s. 4d. He leaves Cromwell and Audeley each a silver cup worth £10, that they may favour the said preachers, so that they may preach these sermons quietly to the laud of God, setting forth the king's godly purposes and extinction of the feigned power of the Bishop of Rome. If it be not permitted in the parish church, then in any other church in London. At the end of every sermon the choir shall sing Te Deum, every priest and clerk singing to have twopence. No bell is to be rung, but only a peal to the sermon, but the clerk and other poor men are to have their duty as if the bell were rung. The will is of some interest, not only as showing the high esteem in which Latimer was held by some, while others abused him as a heretic and longed to see him burnt, but also as indicative of the attitude of certain of the Protestant laity of the day.

Up till this time (1539) the king had on the whole favoured and countenanced the reforming party, and it was not unnatural that they should begin to take it for granted that he would proceed on the same lines. But a blow was awaiting them, all the more overwhelming because it was altogether unexpected. The truth is, the king had personally no very great sympathy with the spirit of the reformers. The Roman Church had interfered with the accomplishment of his private and personal wishes, and he had thrown off its rule. Cranmer was politic and pliable, and had commended himself personally to Henry, and had consequently helped forward the cause of the Reformation. Cromwell had suggested various changes, more especially that of the suppression of monasteries, which commended themselves strongly to the king's cupidity, and had for that reason been carried out with little delay or hesitation. But in all this the keynote of Henry's actions was self-interest; his own supremacy, not the honour of God, was the idea ever before him. In the same year that the Bishops' Book was published negotiations were entered into between the king and certain of the German divines. A deputation of these came over to England, and conferences were held between them and Cranmer. All this pointed to a union between the Reformed Churches, and gave great encouragement to those who had favoured the new learning. But unfortunately the Germans took it upon them to draw up a paper pointing out certain abuses, still prominent in the English Church. These abuses, notably the celibacy of the clergy, private masses, and communion in one kind, they begged the king to reform. It was an unfortunate step to have taken at this particular juncture. The king was no longer in danger of war with Charles, and accordingly no longer dependent on the friendship of the Protestants of Europe. Moreover, he was annoyed by the many reports that came to his ears of lack of reverence on the part of those who favoured the reformed views, reports unfortunately having but too great a foundation of truth; for too many of those of the new faith, in the reaction against excess of ceremony, made fun of and satirised much that pertained to the old religion, composed ballads on the mass, jibed and mocked at what many held to be the most sacred things of religion. Henry was in the state of mind to be lightly roused to violent action, and the protest of the German reformers was all that was needed to make his anger burst forth. Having replied to them directly by the mouth of Tunstal in a style that was far from ingratiating, he proceeded to show his mind yet more strongly by prompt and vigorous action.

In April 1539 the new Parliament met, and the reforming party were startled by a speech which showed that the chief business of Parliament was still to be the settling of religion. He, the king, declared that " he was desirous to have all his subjects of one mind in religion, and to quiet all controversies on the subject, and with this intent he desired his Parliament to appoint a committee to confer upon certain articles, and to bring them before the House." Accordingly a committee was appointed. It consisted of Cromwell and Cranmer and the Bishops of Worcester, Ely, Durham, Bath and Wells, Carlisle, and Bangor—men of such diverse opinions that it was not possible that they should in a short time come to agreement. Certain queries were put to them by the king, the answers to which were to be drawn up in articles. But day after day passed and they were no nearer an agreement than at the beginning, as indeed was to be expected from so strangely mixed a committee. The king would not brook delay, and after eleven days had slipped by, the Duke of Norfolk, acting as the king's spokesman, announced to the House of Lords that as no progress was being made by the committee, it would be well that the matter in dispute should be discussed openly in free Parliament. The questions were then debated with much fire and energy in the House of Lords, the king himself taking part in the discussion. Cranmer strove earnestly, with all the eloquence of which he was undoubtedly master, to prevent the passing of certain of the articles, more especially of that insisting on the celibacy of the clergy, which indeed touched him nearly, as he himself had for some time been married, though his wife, a daughter of the German scholar Osiander, had always been kept in discreet retirement. His opposition, however, prevailed not at all, and on 28th June the Statute of the Six Articles was passed by Parliament. It asserted—(1) That in the most blessed Eucharist the natural body and blood of Christ is present; (2) that communion in both kinds is not needful for all; (3) that priests may not marry; (4) that all vows of chastity must be observed; (5) that private masses were to be commended; (6) that auricular confession is necessary. Those who would not hold the doctrine of transubstantiation were to be punished as heretics by " pain of death by way of burning," with loss of goods as in the case of treason. First offences against the other articles were to involve forfeiture and imprisonment at the will and pleasure of the king; second offences were to entail the death of a felon without clergy. The marriages of priests, or of any man or woman who had vowed chastity or widowhood, were declared void and of none effect; and if any such priest or person who had taken vows of chastity should be found to be married and still living in the married state after the 12th of July, he should be accounted a felon, and suffer accordingly. Abstaining from confession or from communion was held to be an offence against the articles. Special commissions of inquiry were to be instituted, and besides these all bishops and magistrates were authorised to make inquiry, and to take accusations and informations of any offences against the articles. It is not difficult to imagine the dismay and horror of the reformers when this terrible statute became law. Its preamble, expressing a desire for unity, must have seemed a bitter irony, a mockery indeed, to the hundreds, nay thousands, to whose hopes of happiness it came as a deathblow.

It was indeed a cruel Act, and it is clear that even those who had pushed it through Parliament felt it to be extreme and excessive in its cruelty; for although many were imprisoned for disobedience to and non-compliance with its terms, only a small number were actually put to death. Even though its extreme penalties were comparatively seldom carried out, it was a severe blow to the reforming party. The question of the Eucharistic presence was not as yet one which greatly agitated the minds of the reformers. Most men indeed at this time held the old view. Cranmer did not change his position for some little time, and Latimer tells us of himself that it was not till seven years before his death that he adopted the reformed doctrine on this point. But it was very different in regard to the other points dealt with. What was to happen to all those monks and nuns who had been turned out of their monasteries, and who by the consent of silent acquiescence had abandoned their celibate life and entered into the married state? And what of the many priests who were married? The archbishop himself seemed to be in no little danger, and he did not lose any time in sending his wife back to her father in Germany. But Henry loved Cranmer, and indeed found him too useful as an ally easily to let him go from his court, and he sent messengers to him to have no fear, for the king had no evil intentions towards him, but would favour him as he had done hitherto. Even with this assurance it must have been an unpleasant thing for Cranmer to continue the principal officer of a Church which had strongly condemned so much that he approved: it is indeed not very easy to understand how he could remain in his office.

Shaxton and Latimer were clear that they could not retain their offices. In Convocation they had very strongly dissented when the articles were affirmed, and so soon as they became law both bishops resigned their Sees.[1] Shaxton was, according to the law, imprisoned for a little time, in the ward of the Bishop of Bath and Wells. Before very long he forswore the new opinions, and went back to the old religion, preaching at the burning of Anne Askew, and shortly after expressing penitence for all his heresies, in a sermon at Paul's Cross.

It is not quite clear that Latimer had intended to resign at once. Foxe says he did of his own free accord resign and renounce his pastorship, but he himself tells us that he retired at a hint from Cromwell, who told him the king thought it better that he should no longer remain bishop. Afterwards the king disclaimed having spoken to this effect; but Henry not infrequently chose to forget his past

[1] *State Papers* (1539), xiv. i. 1219.

actions. At all events Latimer did resign, and it would even seem that he proposed to leave the country, for as he was going away he was taken at Gravesend or Rochester; he was committed to the care of the Bishop of Chichester, and afterwards imprisoned in the Tower.[1] There he lay for a time, how long it is not easy to discover, looking daily for death.

In one of his sermons, speaking of this time of trouble, he says: "It was objected and said unto me that I was singular, that no man thought as I thought, that I loved a singularity in all that I did, and that I took a way contrary to the king and the whole Parliament, and that I was travailed with them that had better wits than I, that I was contrary to them all. Marry, sir, this was sore thunderbolts. I thought it an irksome thing to be alone and to have no fellow." But in his trouble and loneliness he comforted himself with the thought of his Master, and was at peace.[2]

There was great diversity of opinion among the laity of England in regard to Henry's action. "Never prince showed himself so wise," writes one, "learned, and catholic as the king has done in this Parliament. I cannot express his goodness. We shall have an Act that none shall dare say that bread and wine remains in the sacrament after consecration, nor that priest may have a wife . . . His Highness confounded all with his learning. York, Durham, Winchester, London, Chichester, Norwich, and Carlisle

[1] *State Papers*, xiv. i. 1228. "Bishop Lattomer fledde and is taken at Rochester, and browthe till the Tower."
[2] *Sermons*, p. 136.

have shown themselves honest and well-learned men. We of the temporalty here be all of one opinion, and my Lord Chancellor and Privy Seal as good as we desire. . . . All England is to thank God and most heartily to rejoice of the king's godly proceedings."[1] On the other hand, we have Marillac, the French ambassador, writing to Francis that Henry is "held in distrust by the people on account of religion, in which he makes daily changes. At this last Parliament, to repair past errors and satisfy people and the Christian powers, he has restored all the ancient opinions and constitutions, save obedience to the Pope, and abbeys and churches of which he has taken the revenues. Worcester and Salisbury, chief authors of the new doctrine, have been deprived of their bishoprics for refusing to subscribe to the edict. They have still time to revoke what they have preached if they wish to save their lives."[2] The Germans were of course grieved and distressed. Bucer writes to the Landgrave of Hesse, lamenting the decision of Parliament, and the consequent imprisonment of two of the most pious bishops in England. His account of the state of England is most melancholy. He pictures it as ruled by the "crafty Bishop of Winchester," who has warned the king that if he proceed with the Reformation it will lead to commotion, and the chief nobles of England will be against him. Henry submits to Gardiner because he flatters him with a hope that Francis will join him in deposing the pope, on the understanding that the Reformation shall go no further; the ports are watched that few Protestants may escape, and presently the authorities will proceed to

[1] *State Papers*, xiv. 1040. [2] *Ibid.* xiv. 1260.

extremities with those who are now in prison.[1] These gloomy prognostications were indeed exaggerated, but they were only natural under the circumstances. The German reformers, indeed, were at a loss to understand what Henry meant. "He has spoken much for this learning and condemned France for persecuting it, for he knew it was right. Moreover, he has many pious preachers like the deprived Latimer, and Crome, whom he heard and tolerated for a time. Yet now he denounces these doctrines worse than the Pope, and threatens with death those who do not accept these articles. A terrible persecution has begun." So writes Luther to the Elector of Saxony, concluding with the expression of a fear that Henry cares nothing for the honour of God, but meant to make a religion for himself.[2]

Latimer, on his fall from the high office of a bishop, did not escape abuse, but neither was he lacking in defenders, bold in tongue and quick in retort. Thus, while some rejoiced in his fall and hoped he might get his deserts, a phrase in the mouth of his enemies, meaning that he should be hanged or burnt, there were others, even among those of the triumphant opposition, who called to mind how he was one of the best preachers in Christendom, and mourned over the fact that his successor has never been heard of as a preacher. It was not only those of the new learning who desired reform; there were not a few, even of those who approved the Six Articles, who were fearful lest the result of them might be to land the people in more bondage and blindness than ever. The clearer-sighted could not but perceive that it was bad for the

[1] *State Papers*, xiv. ii. 186.   [2] *Ibid.* xiv. ii. 379.

people when the priests were loth to teach the paternoster in English, when they mocked at it and at the new learning.

Some there were who sneered at the bishops for resigning. "They be not of the wisest sort, for few nowadays will leave and give over such promotions for keeping of opinion."[1] But, again, there were zealous supporters like Dr. Crome, who, careless of himself, boldly preached against the lie-mongers who slandered the bishops, showing that they were men of pure and honest lives, and pointing out that their honesty lay not in their promotions, and did not leave them as some seemed to hold, when they lost their high position.[2]

Henry himself seems to have begun to feel compunctions as to the result of the edict, little favourable to those who have so astutely done this (the edict);[3] certainly, as regards Latimer, he showed himself kindly, for there is evidence that he assured him of a hundred marks pension under the king's broad seal, whether out of his bishopric or from the king's own coffer is uncertain.[4] Melancthon, indeed, took it upon him personally to remonstrate with Henry on his action. He wrote, he said, not so much in the interests of those likeminded with himself, who were in danger by reason of this decree, but rather because he was grieved to think that the king should be minister of such impiety.[5] He hears that Latimer, Shaxton, and Crome are in prison, and would not have the king stain himself with the blood of such men, the lights

---

[1] *State Papers*, xiv. i. 1220.   [2] *Ibid.* xiv. ii. 41.
[3] *Ibid.* xiv. ii. 423. Richardson to Melancthon.
[4] *Ibid.* xiv. ii. 400.   [5] *Ibid.* xiv. ii. 444.

of the Church and the triumph of Antichrist. He subtly indicates that he understands the edict is the act of the king nominally, but of the bishops in reality; and, pointing out the evils which will undoubtedly be the immediate consequence, he begs the king to amend the decree, reminding him that it is never unworthy of a good prince to mitigate unjust severity, upon second thoughts. Melancthon had the character of meek gentleness, but he could speak straight to the point on occasion, as his letter shows. To Cranmer also he wrote on the same subject, not indeed upbraiding or accusing him, for his clear judgment could appraise the difficulties of a man in Cranmer's position, and could perceive the possibility that in his personal action he was taking thought for the welfare and protection of the whole reforming party, rather than of his own private safety or honour, but urging him to see to it that the abuses yet existing in England be reformed, for clearly it was an extraordinary thing to reject the authority and retain the abuses of the Church of Rome. "Wherefore let the simple truth shine forth in the churches, retain the ceremonies divinely given and some useful rites consonant with Holy Writ, let there be moderation, gravity, and elegance, and let not follies be defended which nourish superstition. . . . It is unjust to interpret every violation of such edicts as seditious. If a pious man omit creeping to the cross as superstitious, will you call him seditious if otherwise he is of honest life? It is not expedient to accustom rulers to this new and bitter interpretation of laws. You know the proportion between acts and punishments insisted on by Aristotle, violation of which exposes republics to slavery. I have written at this length not to accuse you but to show my own sorrow."[1] He ends by reverently commending himself to Latimer.

It would seem that after a short imprisonment Latimer retired into private life, somewhere in the country, but that he was not long left in peace. A bishop, possibly Winchester, sent for him and "marvelled that I would not consent to such traditions as were then set out. And I answered him that I would be ruled by God's book, and rather than I would dissent one jot from it I would be torn with wild horses. And I chanced in our communication to name the Lord's Supper. 'Tush,' saith the bishop, 'what do ye call the Lord's Supper? What new term is that?' . . . I made answer that I would rather follow St. Paul in using his terms than them, though they had all the doctors on their side. 'Why,' saith the bishop, 'cannot we, without Scriptures, order the people? How did they before the Scripture was first written and copied out.' But, God knoweth, full ill, yet would they have ordered them, —for seeing that having it, they have deceived us, in what case should we have been now without it?"[2]

In 1546 Crome was called before the Council, and examined for heretical opinions. In the course of his trial it appeared that he had received advice from Latimer which might be deemed heretical, and accordingly Latimer was brought before the Council and examined, but to no effect, for he refused to answer the questions put to him, maintaining that their proceeding was more extreme than if he had lived

[1] *State Papers*, xiv. i. 631. [2] *Sermons*, p. 121.

under the Turk. They told him they were only acting under the king's orders, but he took leave to doubt that statement, saying he had been told it was the king's will that he should resign his bishopric, and found afterwards it was nothing of the kind.[1] Then they reproved him for disrespect, but to this he was indifferent; and being tormented with further questions, he refused to reply save in such wise as to leave the Council no better informed as to what he really thought than they were before. Then he appealed to the king, knowing that he could trust to his support so long as he adhered to the old belief in the matter of transubstantiation; his appeal, says Froude,[2] was allowed, and he was troubled no further. Foxe, on the other hand, says that he was cast into the Tower, where he continually remained prisoner till the time that "blessed King Edward entered his crown." Bernher, Latimer's servant, who preserved and edited many of his sermons, says that he was cast into the Tower, and lay there looking daily for death.[3]

It may be observed that the reaction of this year was not quite so entire as might be thought. The general character of the period may be gathered from the book known as *The Erudition of a Christian Man*, or more popularly the King's Book. Henry had not been fully satisfied with the former book, which had been called the Bishops', and had therefore in 1540 appointed a fresh committee of divines to draw up another guide to doctrine for the benefit of the clergy and the more educated of the people. The

[1] Froude, *History of England*, iv. 495.
[2] *Ibid.* iii. p. 385.   [3] *Sermons*, p. 319.

Erudition is not so different from the *Institution*, as might have been expected from the reactionary views held by the king at the time of its publication. Cranmer still held influence over him, and Cranmer had more to do with this book than anyone else. The king's supremacy is stated much more strongly, and there is throughout the book a more distinctively Erastian tone than is to be observed in the *Institution*. The doctrine of transubstantiation is stated more strongly, the invocation of saints is encouraged, and the marriage of priests forbidden, but Rome is strongly condemned, and, as a whole, the book is confessedly a reforming work. In his preface Henry said he had had the advice of his clergy, but as he was well known to have himself had much to do with its construction, or rather compilation, it became commonly known as the King's Book, and as such received the approval of Convocation, though this was now hardly more than a matter of form; for Parliament had in 1540 passed an Act ruling that whatever should be agreed on by the committee of divines appointed, and allowed by the king, must be believed and accepted by all the king's subjects. Another excellent bit of work done by Cranmer at the command of the king was the translating and altering of the old Latin Litany, the first model of the present office. This was to be used in the churches on festival days. He also persuaded the king to order certain ceremonies to be disused, such as the creeping to the cross and vigils, as they engendered much superstition in the minds of the common people. Thus mainly by means of Cranmer things were made ready for the more complete readjustment possible on the accession of the young Protestant prince. We may find it difficult to understand how Cranmer held on in his position, but undoubtedly had he withdrawn and left the conduct of affairs to Gardiner, the Reformation settlement might have been very considerably retarded.

CHAPTER IV

WITH the accession of Edward VI. the power passed into the hands of a strong Protestant party, led by the uncle of the young king. By Act of Parliament Henry was authorised to leave the crown by will, according as he saw fit. His idea seems to have been to hedge round his young son with counsellors carefully chosen from the rival parties in such wise that his own policy might be carried on much in the same fashion as in his lifetime, until such time as Edward was fit to take the reins into his own hands. But Henry might have foreseen what would happen, had he only looked ahead a little. No sooner was he dead than the Earl of Hertford, the maternal uncle of the king, took the control of everything, by rapid action managed to have himself appointed Lord Protector during the minority of the king, became Duke of Somerset, and proceeded to govern the country with the assistance of the Council. The more conservative members of Council were before very long ejected, and Somerset addressed himself, with the ill-considered haste of a rash and revolutionary spirit, to attack and overcome all the difficulties involved in his position. There were strained relations between England and Scotland, difficulties with Germany and France, trouble between the richer and poorer classes of the country, and a complicated and intricate financial problem to solve. With a light heart Somerset faced them, one and all, confident in himself, in his good intentions and his eminent capacity for any and every thing.

The brothers of Jane Seymour had always belonged to the strong Protestant party, and the new rule meant, of course, the complete re-establishment of the power of Cranmer and the rapid promotion of the Reformation. It is not necessary, in a Life of Latimer, to enter into the history of the development of Protestantism in the English Church, more especially as Latimer either was not asked to accept, or, if asked, refused any official position under the new Government. Heath, the new Bishop of Worcester, was much afraid lest Latimer should dispossess him, and his fears were justified by the action of the Commons, who presented an address to the Protector, asking him to restore Latimer, which he would gladly have done; but the old man refused, thinking himself no longer fit for the arduous labours of a bishop, thinking, too, that his restitution would be a little hard on Heath.[1] He returned to public life in the year 1547 as a licensed preacher, occupying a position of great importance in the country, in some ways indeed of greater importance than before, not merely theologically, though it would seem that Cranmer closely consulted him in the matter of the Authorised Homilies, but more particularly as a candid though friendly critic of all the actions of the Government. Cranmer apparently invited him to stay with him at Lambeth, and here he lived quietly, appealed to

[1] Dixon, iii. 9.

by all kinds of people for every manner of redress and help—by the poor and needy in all parts of England, and by foreigners of all kinds, distinguished and unimportant. "I cannot go to my book, for poor folks come unto me desiring me that I will speak that their matters may be heard. I trouble my lord of Canterbury, and being at his house, now and then I walk in the garden looking in my book, as I can do but little good at it. . . . I am no sooner in the garden and have read awhile, but by and by cometh there some one or other knocking at the gate. . . . When I come there then it is some one or other that desireth me that I will speak that his matter might be heard."[1] Fortunately a great number of the sermons of this period have been preserved us. The great interest pertaining to these is not so much theological as practical, and in connection with the social condition of the country. They bring out therefore, perhaps more clearly than had before appeared, Latimer's position as a practical reformer of manners and morals, and more especially his genuine interest in the condition of the agricultural classes in the country. In 1548 he began a series of sermons on the crying evils of the age, delivered at St. Paul's Cross, and in the spring of the same year he was appointed to preach the Lenten sermons before the king. These last he delivered from a pulpit erected in the king's garden, repeating the Lord's Prayer in English both before and after the sermon. This was his general custom in these days, and he tells us he did it with the intention that the people might become familiar with

[1] *Sermons*, p. 127.

the prayer; for he found that many of those who came to him seeking alms were quite ignorant of it, telling him they could repeat the old paternoster, that is the Latin, but not the new, that is the English.[1] It would be very easy to find fault with these sermons of Latimer's, from a literary point of view. They are, indeed, rough and rambling, and even incoherent at times, but there is a genuine vigour and force of language, and a simplicity and earnestness which bespeak the conviction of the preacher; and, after all, sermons are not literary productions but words spoken for the need of the moment, and it was the actual evils of the moment which Latimer attacked, it was from the fulness of his heart that his mouth spoke; and, as a natural consequence, his words roused a response in the hearts of his hearers; his preaching was effective beyond any power of mere fine literary writing.

We have now come to a time when a certain feature of the social condition of England began to be very conspicuous, the distressed state, that is, of the labourers and small farmers. Since the middle of the fifteenth century the country had been passing through not only a religious and political, but also a great social and industrial revolution. The prosperity of the small farmer and the labourer had gradually but steadily declined. This was in great part due to the enormous development of the wool trade with the Netherlands, and the consequent withdrawal of much of the land from purposes of agriculture to those of mere pasturage, in part to the new relations between the owners of land and the tenants. The later feudal system was dying out, and the old ties binding rich

[1] *Sermons* "at Stamford," p. 307.

and poor together were loosened, and no fresh bonds were yet formed to take their place. No doubt the old system was full of drawbacks, chief among which was the great danger of abuse of power on the part of the nobles; but, granting all the disadvantages, it bound the State together with no ordinary strength. In the sixteenth century it became the fashion for the great London merchants to buy lands in the country, and they brought with them their more commercial views of life, not altogether to the advantage of the country people.

But no doubt the great trouble was the conversion of a large portion of what had been arable to mere pasture land, with the consequence that in many places where there had been large and thriving villages inhabited by numbers of labourers, able after a fashion at least to maintain their wives and families, there were now a mere handful of shepherds to look after the great flocks of sheep which inhabited the land. As a result, the country was filled with a huge army of unemployed, who drifted towards the large towns seeking to find some work, or hung about in the country, subsisting for the most part on charity. This drifting, shifting population was an evil which the Government had now to face. Henry VIII. had passed various Acts, which were intended to correct this state of affairs, but without much result. Now, again, under Somerset a new and severer Vagrancy Act was passed, ordering that any determinedly idle and able-bodied vagrant might be adjudged by two magistrates to any one wanting him as a slave, branded with the letter V, and kept a slave for two years. If he still refused to work, he might be made a slave for life, or even punished as a felon. The Government, indeed, did not know how to cope with the trouble; they were hopelessly at a loss, and strove by severe measures to accomplish something. So severe an Act as this could not long continue in force; two years only had passed before it was repealed, and even while it was in existence it was not, for it could not be, fully enforced. It was hard to punish men for not working, when in truth the only kind of labour for which they were fitted had been taken from them by what might be called natural forces. The State at various times tried by artificial means to promote various industries, as, for example, when the statute was enacted for the "encouragement of linen trade, the better employment of the people, and the avoidance of the sin of idleness." "Every person occupying land for tillage shall, for every sixty acres which he hath under the plough, sow one quarter of an acre in flax or hemp." But such laws inevitably had little result, for they did not reach to the root of the evil, and served but to tinker up a system which it was necessary thoroughly to reconstruct. Another woe threatened the unfortunate labourer. Not only was much of what had hitherto been arable land turned into pasture, but the ancient rights of the people in regard to the unenclosed commons were invaded. The landlords began to enclose and take in great tracts of the common lands which existed to no inconsiderable extent all over England, and which had hitherto provided the labourer with great part of his livelihood. As was very natural, the people were filled with discontent and resentment; they could not find work, and their old-time rights were no longer preserved. Whether, indeed, Somerset was inspired by a genuine sympathy with and pity for the sufferings which made themselves known by the bitter cry of many, or whether, as has been suggested, he was merely prompted by the desire to figure as a patriot, at all events, instead of issuing fresh and severer laws of repression, he instituted a Commission to inquire into and redress this great evil, at the same time opening in his own house a Court of Requests, where the poor might plead their wrongs and hope for more speedy attention.[1] In his second sermon before Edward, Latimer speaks of the delay which poor men suffer from, and begs the king to hear their causes himself.

"The saying is now that money is heard everywhere; if he be rich, he shall soon have an end of his matter. Others are fain to go home with weeping tears, for any help they can obtain at any judge's hand. Hear men's suits yourself, I require you in God's behalf, and put it not to the hearing of these velvet coats—these upskips. . . . View your judges and hear poor men's causes."[2]

In a proclamation issued on the 1st of June 1549 Somerset explained the necessity for immediate action of some kind. "By the enclosing of lands and arable grounds many have been driven to extreme poverty, and compelled to leave the places where they were born. Ten, twenty, or a hundred Christian people have been inhabiting and keeping households where now there is nothing but sheep or bullocks. All the land which was occupied heretofore with so many men and furnished so many markets is now gotten by

[1] Dixon, ii. p. 506. [2] *Sermons*, p. 127.

insatiable greediness into the hands of one or two men, and scarcely dwelt upon with one poor shepherd. The insatiable covetousness of men encroaches daily; the realm is brought to a marvellous desolation. Houses are decayed, parishes diminished, the poor forced to lead an idle and loitering life. The cattle belonging to so few, the cattle which have driven so many from their homes, are gathered in great flocks and droves, whence rots and murrains come among them; nor are they so cheap as they would be dispersed in many hands; for these men hold them dear, and are able to tarry the advantage of the market."[1] The Commission showed what had been done in the past to check the evil; how laws had been made to promote husbandry, to discourage the plurality of farms, to maintain hospitality on the sites of the dissolved monasteries. But all efforts had been vain; the laws had not been executed, chiefly because of the general corruption and love of money; the realm was decayed and the people oppressed. The most energetic member of the Commission, and very possibly the real promoter of the whole movement, was John Hales, Clerk of the Hanaper, a zealous reformer and favourer of the new learning.[2] He was fully conversant with, and full of pity for, the unhappy condition of the people, and showed an extraordinary energy and activity as a commissioner, trying by every means in his power to make the inquiry really useful. In the charge with which he was wont to begin his interrogations he attributes the greater part of the existing evil to the "dropsy of riches, the insatiate

[1] Dixon, ii. pp. 506, 507.
[2] *Ibid.* pp. 508, 509.

desire of gain . . . the filthy desire of getting together goods." As to an enclosure: "where a man doth enclose and hedge his own proper ground where no man hath common, this is beneficial to the commonwealth; . . ." but what men have done is that they have "taken away and enclosed others' commons, or have pulled down houses of husbandry, and converted tillage to pasture." His zeal roused the wrath of the nobles, who declared that his purpose was to stir up the poor against the gentry. Hales denied this, but urged them to have compassion on the poor, "for the sore is brought to such extremity that if it be not remedied all the realm shall rue." In his sermons before the king and at Paul's Cross Latimer vehemently discoursed on the same theme. Reminding the king of the text, "He shall not multiply unto himself too much gold and silver," he says: "I doubt most rich men have too much; for without too much we can get nothing. As, for example, the physician; if the poor man be diseased he can have no help without too much; and of the lawyer, the poor man can get no counsel, expedition, nor help in his matter, except he give him too much. At merchants' hands no kind of ware can be had except we give for it too much. You landlords, you rent-raisers, I may say you step-lords, you unnatural lords, you have for your possessions yearly too much. For that here before went for twenty or forty pound by year (which is an honest portion to be had gratis in one lordship of another man's sweat and labour) now is let for fifty or an hundred pound by year. Of this 'too much' cometh this monstrous and portentous dearth made by man, notwithstanding God doth send us plentifully the fruits of the earth, mercifully, contrary unto our deserts; notwithstanding, too much, which these rich men have, causeth such dearth that poor men which live of their labour cannot with the sweat of their face have a living, all kind of victuals is so dear—pigs, geese, capons, chickens, eggs, etc. Those things with others are so unreasonably enhanced, and I think verily that if it thus continue we shall at length be constrained to pay for a pig a pound. . . . I will tell you, my lords and masters, this is not for the king's honour. . . . If the king's honour, as some men say, standeth in the great multitude of people, then the graziers, meloners, and rent-rearers are hinderers of the king's labour. For where as have been a great many householders and inhabitants there is now but a shepherd and his dog; so they hinder the king's honour most of all. . . ." He goes on to show how the position of the yeoman has sunk in his lifetime. " My father," he says, " was a yeoman, and had no lands of his own, only he had a farm of three or four pound by year at the uttermost, and hereupon he tilled so much as kept half a dozen men. He had walk for a hundred sheep; and my mother milked thirty kine. He was able and did find the king a harness, with himself and his horse, while he came to the place that he should receive the king's wages. . . . He kept me to school, or else I had not been able to have preached before the King's Majesty now. He married my sisters with five pound or twenty nobles apiece; so that he brought them up in godliness and fear of God. He kept hospitality for his poor neighbours, and some alms he gave to the poor. And all this he did of the said farm, where he that now hath it payeth sixteen pound by year or more, and is not able to do anything for his prince, for himself, nor for his children, or give a cup of drink to the poor. Thus all the enhancing and rearing goeth to your private commodity and wealth. So that where ye had a single too much you have that, and since the same ye have enhanced the rent and so have increased another too much: so now ye have double too much, which is too too much. But let the preacher preach till his tongue be worn to the stumps, nothing is amended. We have good statutes made for the commonwealth as touching commoners and inclosers, many meetings and sessions, but in the end of the matter there cometh nothing forth. Well, this is one thing I will say unto you: from whence this cometh I know, even from the devil. I know his intent in it; for if ye bring it to pass that the yeomanry be not able to put their sons to school . . . and that they be not able to marry their daughters, ye pluck salvation from the people, and utterly destroy the realm. For by yeomen's sons the faith of Christ is and hath been maintained chiefly."[1] His hope is that the bitter cry of the poor will penetrate to the heart of the king, and that, when he comes of age, he will redress their woes.

The enhancement of rents was but a natural consequence of all that had gone before. New landlords cared little for the claims of old tenants, and were anxious only to get as high a rent as possible for their land. The whole country was permeated by the commercial spirit, the desire to make money, the curse of covetousness.

"Beware of covetousness," preached Latimer. "At the preaching of Jonas the people of Nineve believed

[1] *Sermons*, pp. 99–102.

God and were converted from their sin. This was a great fruit; for Jonas was but one man and he preached but one sermon, and it was but a short sermon neither, as touching the number of words, and yet he turned all the whole city, great and small, rich and poor, king and all. We be many preachers here in England, and we preach many long sermons, yet the people will not repent or convert . . . A strange matter, so noble a city to give place to one man's sermon! Now England cannot abide this gear; they cannot be content to hear God's minister and his threatening for their sin, though the sermon be never so good, though it be never so true. It is a naughty fellow, a seditious fellow; he maketh trouble and rebellion in the realm, he lacketh discretion . . . Nowadays if they cannot reprove the doctrine that is preached, then they will reprove the preacher, that he lacketh due consideration of the times, and that he is of learning sufficient, but he wanteth discretion. . . . I will now ask you a question: I pray you, when should Jonas have preached against the covetousness of Nineve if the covetous men should have appointed him his time? I know that preachers ought to have a discretion in their preaching, and that they ought to have a consideration and respect to the place and the time that he preacheth in. But sin must be rebuked; sin must be plainly spoken against. . . . Nineve shall arise against England because it will not believe God nor hear His preachers that cry daily unto them, nor amend their lives, and especially their covetousness."[1]

"Therefore, you preachers, out with your swords and

[1] *Sermons*, pp. 239, etc.

strike at the root. Speak against covetousness and cry out upon it. Stand not ticking and toying at the branches nor at the boughs, for then there will new boughs and branches spring again of them; but strike at the root and fear not these giants of England, these great men and men of power, these men that are oppressors of the poor; fear them not, but strike at the root of all evil which is mischievous covetousness. For covetousness is the cause of rebellion. I have forgotten my logic, but yet I can jumble at a syllogism and make an argument of it, to prove it by. Covetousness is the root of all evil; rebellion is an evil; ergo, covetousness is the root of rebellion. And so it was indeed. Covetousness was the cause of rebellion this last summer, and both parties had covetousness, as well the gentlemen as the commons . . . both parties had an inordinate desire to have that they had not. . . . The commons thought they had a right to the things that they inordinately sought to have. But what then? They must not come to it that way. Now, on the other side, the gentlemen had a desire to keep that they had . . . and thus both parties had covetousness, and both parties did rebel."[1] And again, "I read of late in an Act of Parliament, and this Act made mention of an Act that was in King Henry's day: In this Parliament that I speak of, the gentlemen that were landlords would needs have away much lands from their tenants and would needs have an Act of Parliament that it might be lawful for them to inclose and make several from their tenants and from the commons such portions of their lands as they thought good.

[1] *Sermons*, p. 247.

Much ado there was about this Act, at last it was concluded and granted that they might do so; provided alway that they should leave sufficient to the tenant. Well, it was well that they were bound to leave sufficient for them. But who should be the judge to limit what is sufficient. . . . And then fell I to make this argument within myself: if at that time it were put in their will and power that they might inclose, leaving to the tenant that were sufficient for him; if they had it then in their power, thought I, that they might this do, they would leave no more than sufficient. If they left to the tenants and poor commons no more in those days but sufficient; then if they had any more taken from them since that time, then had they now not sufficient. They in Christ are equal with you. The poorest ploughman is in Christ equal with the greatest prince that is. Let them therefore have sufficient to maintain them and to find them their necessaries. . . . They must have sheep . . . to help to fat the land, or they shall have but bare corn and thin. They must have swine for their food . . . for bacon is their necessary meat to feed on, which they may not lack; . . . they must have other cattle, as horses to draw their plough . . . and kine for their milk and cheese, which they must live upon and pay their rents. These cattle must have pasture, which pasture if they lack the rest must needs fail them, and pasture they cannot have if the land be taken in and inclosed from them. Therefore, for God's love, restore their sufficient unto them . . . and beware of covetousness."[1] He begins and ends with the same warn-

[1] *Sermons*, pp. 248–250.

ing, and repeats it again and again in the course of his sermons. The cry of the poor is ever in his ears, and will not be silenced. "The workmen make their moan that they can get no money. The poor labourers, gunmakers, powder-men, bow-makers, arrow-makers, smiths, carpenters, soldiers, and other crafts, cry out for their duties. They be unpaid, some of them, three or four months; yea some of them half a year; yea some of them put up bills this time twelve months for their money and cannot be paid yet. They cry out for their money, and as the prophet says, 'The cry of the workmen is come up to mine ears.' O! for God's love let the workmen be paid, if there be money enough, or else there will whole showers of God's vengeance rain down upon your heads."[1] Again: "For God's sake make some promoters" (informers who prosecuted offenders against the laws). "There lack men to punish the king's officers when they do amiss, and to promote all offenders. I think there is great need of such men of godly discretion, wisdom, and conscience to promote transgressors, as rent-raisers, oppressors of the poor, extortioners, bribers, usurers. I hear there be usurers in England, that will take forty in the hundred, but I hear of no promoters to put them up. We read not, this covetous farmer or landed man of the gospel bought corn in the markets to lay it up in store, and then sell it again. But I hear say that in England we have landlords, nay step-lords, I may say, that are become graziers; and burgesses are become regraters and some farmers will regrate and buy up all the corn that cometh to the markets and lay it up in store and sell it again at a

[1] *Sermons*, pp. 261, 262.

higher price, when they see their time.[1] . . . Yea, and aldermen nowadays are become colliers; they be both woodmongers and makers of coal. . . . There cannot a poor body buy a sack of coals, but it must come through their hands. . . ." Latimer does not by any means despise riches or think that to be wealthy is necessarily to be wicked. " God giveth men plenty of riches to exercise their faith and charity, to confirm them that be good, to draw them that he naught, and to bring them to repentance, and the devil worketh altogether to the contrary . . . I do not despise riches, but I wish that men should have riches as Abraham had, and as Joseph had. A man to have riches to help his neighbour is godly riches. The worldly riches is to put all his trust and confidence in his worldly riches, that he may by them live gallantly, pleasantly, and voluptuously."[2] John Hales was as vehement as Latimer in denouncing the custom of regrating and forcing the market. He brought in three Bills for the relief of the poor, and in supporting these Bills in Parliament declared that he knew of a certainty that graziers and sheepmasters went to market taking with them cattle and money. If they failed to sell their cattle for as high a price as they considered they ought to fetch, they refused to sell at all, but, instead, bought up all other cattle in the market and went home. These having raised the market, within a few days they sold at their own price. As to the cause of the trouble in the country, Hales was in perfect agreement with Latimer, and spoke with equal force and vehemence. "Man is become a wolf, a devourer and consumer, that will not

[1] *Sermons*, p. 279.   [2] *Ibid.* p. 280.

let his neighbours live. There is dearth and scarceness of victual without just cause. . . . Men are drowned in this filthy desire of getting together goods."[1]

Whatever the causes, there can be no doubt as to the fact that the condition of the agricultural and labouring population was rapidly declining, and as a natural result the whole country was in a state of dangerous ferment, the common people boldly talking of claiming their rights and putting down enclosures, while the expelled priests and all the many hangers-on of the monasteries added to the general moan and complaint.

The dissolution of the monasteries was certainly one cause of the increase of vagabonds and beggars. Howsoever we may deplore the probably unsatisfactory state of some of the religious houses, and the general carelessness of the great majority of them, it cannot be denied that, as a rule, the virtue of hospitality was not forgotten by the monks, and in most cases they gave much to the poor. Very probably their fashion of giving was not very wise, and much is to be said against the habit of maintaining a number of idle and useless hangers-on; but be that as it may, the monasteries, as a rule, were institutions of charity, and their dissolution threw upon the country the need of providing charitable relief. What was, however, much worse than the dissolution of the monasteries was the confiscation of the guild property in the county towns and in the country. King Henry had received from Parliament the power of suppressing colleges, hospitals, chantries, and other corporations of the kind, and had exercised his power to some considerable

[1] Hales charge when acting as Commissioner, Dixon, ii. p. 509.

extent. But the great mass of these religious foundations remained untouched at his death.[1] A new Act was passed early in Edward's reign, giving the young king the same power of confiscation as his father had had. The property was not nearly so great in amount as that confiscated by the dissolution of the monasteries, but Cranmer and others of the reforming bishops were strong in opposition to the Bill. Cranmer thought that the chantry lands should rather be devoted to increasing the value of the poorer livings, and he urged that at anyrate the matter might be left over till the king was of age. But the Act was carried none the less. It reached beyond the merely clerical corporations, and laid a hand on the property of all guilds, fraternities, and companies, whether lay or clerical, thus emphasising the fact continually reiterated by Latimer, that covetousness on the part of the wealthy and powerful was the real root of the trouble in the country. The guilds were wealthy, and were a safeguard to the poor; and now they were all to be made over to the king. These guilds and fraternities were the great friendly societies of the time, the only insurances for old age and sickness attainable by the poorer classes. As they were connected with the religious institutions, it was not difficult to persuade men they were superstitious and undesirable; the real truth being that the Government could not know of such wealthy bodies without desiring to take possession of their store. This grasping at the riches of the guilds was one chief cause of the great rising in Norfolk in 1549, to deal with which so greatly perplexed the Lord Protector. His sympathies were with the rebels,

[1] Dixon, ii. p. 460.

who desired merely social reforms, such as he himself had strongly advocated. He found it very hard to know how to act; for however much he might sympathise with the motives of the rebels, he could hardly countenance their lawlessness, and if he punished them with the leniency he felt inclined to, he could hardly treat with severity the other rebels in the West; yet with these he had no sympathy, their complaints being largely of the new ecclesiastical regulations which he himself had helped to enact. Overwhelmed by his many difficulties, he hesitated and wavered, showing in this emergency the weakness of his character, and thereby forfeiting his right to his high position. The Council took the matter into their own hands, crushed the rebellion both in the East and in the West, and re-established peace in England.

By the fall of Somerset the power passed into the hands of Warwick and his friends in the Council. Somerset was weak, indeed, and too desirous of popularity, but some of his intentions at least were excellent, and he had a good deal of sympathy with the wrongs of the common people. Warwick, who now came into power, had no particular aspirations beyond his own advancement, no special principles of any kind. He and his friends were open to persuasion when it came in the form of bribery. Instead of things being better than under Somerset, they were rather worse. And added to all the other troubles came a very real difficulty in the question of the currency. Henry had largely depreciated the coin in his day, and his example had been followed by Somerset, whose many plans involved a considerable expenditure of money, and who found the easiest way to obtain the necessary funds was to debase the coin. The natural result was of course an enormous increase in prices, and once more it was the poor who suffered.

All these various ills from which the country suffered were dealt with vigorously by Latimer. If we take his famous sermon "on the Plough," along with the series of eight sermons preached before the king, to which we have already alluded, we shall get another very vivid picture of the times. He spares none, but inveighs against all the prevalent abuses and superstitions. The picture he draws is terribly sad, a picture of the decline of morals, of the entire corruption of society. "What shall I say of these rich citizens of London? Is there not reigning in London as much pride, as much covetousness, as much cruelty, as much oppression, as much superstition as was in Nebo? Yes, I think, and much more too. Therefore I say repent, oh London, repent, repent! . . . And you rulers and officers, be wise and circumspect, look to your charge, and see you do your duties; and rather be glad to amend your ill-living than to be angry when you are warned of your fault.[1] . . . Burgesses of London — nay, butterflies. . . . Yet, would God they were no worse than butterflies! Butterflies do but their nature; the butterfly is not covetous, is not greedy of other men's goods, is not full of envy and hatred, is not malicious, is not cruel, is not merciless. . . . If I might see any such inclination in you, that you would leave to be merciless and begin to be charitable, I would then hope well of you; I would then speak well of you. But London was never so ill as it is now. In times past men were

[1] *Sermons*, p. 64.

full of pity and compassion, but now there is no pity; for in London their brother shall die in the streets for cold, he shall lie sick at the door between stock and stock, I cannot tell what to call it, and perish there for hunger. ... Now charity is waxen cold, none helpeth the scholar nor yet the poor."

The universities were in a state of decay, and there were none to help. "In times past when any rich man died in London, they were wont to help the poor scholars of the universities with exhibitions. When any man died, they would bequeath great sums of money toward the relief of the poor. When I was a scholar in Cambridge myself, I heard very good report of London, and knew many that had relief of the rich men of London, but now I can hear no such good report, and yet I inquire of it and hearken for it. But now charity is waxen cold, none helpeth the scholar nor yet the poor. And in those days what did they when they helped the scholars? Marry, they maintained and gave them livings that were very papists and professed the pope's doctrine; and now that the knowledge of God's word is brought to light, and many earnestly study and labour to set it forth, now almost no man helpeth to maintain them."[1]

"Why are not the noblemen and young gentlemen of England so brought up in knowledge of God, and in learning, that they may be able to execute offices in the common-weal? The king hath a great many of wards, and I trow there is a Court of Wards; why is there not a school for the wards as well as there is a Court for their lands? Why are they not set in

[1] *Sermons* "on the Plough," pp. 64, 65.

schools where they may learn? Or why are they not sent to the universities, that they may be able to serve the king when they come to age? If the wards and young gentlemen were well brought up in learning and in the knowledge of God, they would not, when they come to age, so much give themselves to other vanities. And if the nobility be well trained in godly learning, the people would follow the same train. For truly, such as the noblemen be, such will the people be. And now, the only reason why noblemen be not made lord presidents is because they have not been brought up in learning. Therefore, for the love of God, appoint teachers and schoolmasters, you that have charge of youth, and give the teachers stipends worthy their pains that they may bring them up in grammar, in logic, in rhetoric, in philosophy, in the civil law, and in that which I cannot leave unspoken of, the word of God."[1] Latimer is careful to explain that he does not mean to insinuate that all the nobility are ignorant and uneducated, only he would have them all more highly trained for the service of the State. In a sermon preached at Stamford he returns to the subject: "Schools are not maintained; scholars have not exhibition, the preaching office decayeth; men provide lands and riches for their children, but this most necessary office they for the most part neglect. Very few there be that help poor scholars, that set their children to school to learn the word of God and to make a provision for the age to come."[2] "It would pity a man's heart to hear that, that I hear of the state of Cambridge; what it is in Oxford I cannot tell.

[1] *Sermons* "on the Plough," p. 69.
[2] *Sermons*, p. 291.

There be few do study divinity, but so many as of necessity must furnish the colleges, for their livings be so small and victuals so dear. . . . It will come to pass that we shall have nothing but a little English divinity that will bring the realm into a very barbarousness and utter decay of learning. It is not that, I wis, that will keep out the supremacy of the Bishop of Rome. Here I will make a supplication that ye would bestow so much to the finding of scholars of good wits, of poor men's sons, to exercise the office of salvation, in relieving of scholars, as ye were wont to bestow in pilgrimage matters, in trentals, in masses, in pardons, in purgatory matters. . . . You may be sure if you bestow your goods on this wise ye shall bestow it well, to support and uphold God's word; wherein ye shall please God. . . . There be none now but great men's sons in colleges, and their fathers look not to have them preachers; so every way this office of preaching is pinched at." [1] . . .

Again, "But this much I say unto you, magistrates, if ye will not maintain schools and universities, ye shall have a brutality. Therefore now a suit again to your Highness. So order the matter that preaching may not decay; for surely if preaching decay, ignorance and brutishness will enter again. Nor give the preachers' livings to secular men. What should the secular men do with the livings of preachers? I think there be at this day ten thousand students less than were within these twenty years, and fewer preachers; and that is the cause of rebellion. If there were good bishops there should be no rebellion." [2]

[1] *Sermons*, p. 179.
[2] *Ibid.* p. 269.

Another matter of which Latimer complains was that the judges were corrupt, and open to bribery from anyone. "They will be waged by the rich, either to give sentence against the poor, or to put off the poor man's causes. This is the noble theft of princes and of magistrates. They are bribe-takers. Nowadays they call them gentle rewards: let them leave their colouring, and call them by their Christian name, bribes. ... We be far worse than those stiff-necked Jews. For we read of none of them that winced nor kicked against Esay's preaching, or said that he was a seditious fellow. ... It is very sure that they that be good will bear and not spurn at the preachers; they that be faulty, they must amend, and neither spurn nor wince nor whine. He that findeth himself touched or galled, he declareth himself not to be upright ... They follow bribes. Somewhat was given to them before, and they must needs give somewhat again; for Giffe-gaffe was a good fellow: this Giffe-gaffe led them clean from justice."[1] The king is responsible, says Latimer. "If the king and his Council should suffer evil judges of this realm to take bribes, to defeat justice, and suffer the great to overgo the poor, and should look through his fingers and wink at it, should not the king be partaker of their naughtiness? And why? Is he not supreme head of the Church? What is the supremacy—a dignity, and nothing else? Is it not accountable? I think it will be a chargeable dignity when account shall be asked of it."[2]

Again: "I am sure this is *scala inferni*, the right way to hell, to take bribes, and pervert justice. If a

[1] *Sermons*, p. 139.   [2] *Ibid.* p. 152.

judge should ask me the way to hell, I would show him the way: first let him be a covetous man, let his heart be poisoned with covetousness; then let him go a little further and take bribes, and last, pervert judgment. . . . There lacks a fourth to make up the mess, which (so God help me), if I were judge, should be *hangum tuum*, a Tyburn tippet to take with him, and it were the Judge of the King's Bench, my Lord Chief Judge of England: yea, and it were my Lord Chancellor himself, to Tyburn with him." Here, after his usual custom, he interpolates anecdotes. Then " I would wish that of such a judge (of a corrupt judge that is) in England now we might have the skin hanged up. It were a goodly sign, the sign of the judge's skin. It should be Lot's wife to all judges that should follow after." [1]

If the judges were corrupt, the clergy were no better. "They will be lords and no labourers when they are commanded to go and be resident upon their cures, and preach in their benefices.[2] They would say, 'What! I have set a deputy there.' . . . And what a deputy must he be, trow ye? Even one like himself; he must be a canonist, that is to say, one that is brought up in the study of the pope's laws and decrees; one that will set forth papistry as well as himself will do, and one that will maintain all superstition and idolatry. . . .

"But in the meantime the prelates take their pleasures. They are lords and no labourers, but the devil is diligent at his plough. . . . The people must have meat that must be familiar and continual, and daily given unto them to feed upon. Many make a

[1] *Sermons*, pp. 179–181.   [2] *Sermons*, p. 77.

strawberry of it, ministering it but once a year, but such do not the office of good prelates. . . . How few there be throughout this realm that give meat to their flock as they should do, the Visitors can best tell." [1]

"But now for the fault of unpreaching prelates, methink I could guess what might be said for excusing of them. They are so troubled with lordly living; they be so placed in palaces, couched in courts, ruffling in their rents, dancing in their dominions, burdened with ambassages, pampering of their paunches, like a monk that maketh his jubilee; munching in their mangers, and moiling in their gay manors and mansions, and so troubled with loitering in their lordships that they cannot attend it. They are otherwise occupied; some in the king's matters, some are ambassadors, some of the Privy Council, some to furnish the Court, some are lords of the Parliament, some are Presidents and Comptrollers of Mints. Well, well, is this their duty? Is this their calling? Should we have ministers of the Church to be Comptrollers of the Mints? Is this a meet office for a priest that hath cure of souls? Is this his charge? I would here ask one question. I would fain know who controlleth the devil at home in his parish while he controlleth the mint? . . . I cannot tell you, but the saying is that since priests have been ministers, money hath been worse than it was before. And they say that the evilness of money hath made all things dearer." [2]

"I will be a suitor to your grace," he says to the king on another occasion, "that ye will give your

[1] *Sermons*, p. 62.   [2] *Ibid.* pp. 67, 68.

bishops charge ere they go home, upon their allegiance, to look better to their flock, and to see your majesty's *Injunctions* better kept, and send your Visitors in their tails; and if they be found negligent or faulty in their duties, out with them. I require it in God's name, make them quondams, all the pack of them."[1] No wonder Latimer had his enemies. Speech of this kind was not calculated to please the clergy, nor could they have liked his bold assertion that the king need have no fear of being unable to fill up the places of the unpreaching prelates; for "there is in this realm, thanks be to God, a great sight of laymen, well learned in the Scriptures, and of virtuous and godly conversations, better learned than a great sight of us of the clergy." These, he declared, would be quite fit, and some of them ready enough, to do the work of the prelates; let them have institution, and turn out the idlers. He was not suffered to preach thus boldly without some remonstrance from his fellows of the clergy. After the sermon just quoted from, a bishop came to him and expressed himself with some indignation, and suggested that Latimer was a quondam himself, and hence it was that he was desirous to see other bishops in a like position.[2] "As for my quondamship," said Latimer in his next sermon, for he generally took an opportunity of replying publicly to any such private accusations, "I thank God He gave me the grace to come by it by so honest a means as I did; I thank Him for mine own quondamship, and as for them I would not have them made quondams if they discharge their duty. I would have them do their duty; I

[1] *Sermons*, p. 122.   [2] *Ibid.* p. 154.

would have no more quondams, as God help me. I owe them no more malice than this, and that is none at all."[1]

Another person accused him of being a seditious fellow for speaking as he did of the coinage. "I chanced," says Latimer, "to speak a merry word of the new shilling, to refresh my auditory, how I was like to put away my new shilling for an old groat. I was herein noted to speak seditiously. Yet I comfort myself in one thing, that I am not alone, and that I have a fellow. . . . Wot ye who is my fellow? The prophet Esayas, He was bold to speak to Jerusalem and to meddle with their coin. 'Thy silver,' he said, 'is turned into dross.' Ah! seditious wretch, what had he to do with the mint? . . . Marry, he espied a piece of divinity in that policy . . . he went to the root of the matter, which was covetousness. . . . As he said to the Jews, 'Thy wine is mingled with water,' so might he have said to us of this land, 'Thy cloth is mingled with flock - powder.'" Latimer here refers to another of the crying evils of the time, to correct which several Acts of Parliament were passed, both in the reign of Henry and of Edward. "I hear say there is a certain cunning come up in mixing of wares. How say you? Were it no wonder to hear that cloth-makers should become poticaries? . . . If his cloth be seventeen yards long, he will set him on a rack, and stretch him out with ropes, and rack him till the sinews stretch again while he hath brought him to eighteen yards. When they have brought him to that perfection, they have a pretty feat to thick him again.

[1] *Sermons*, p. 154.

He makes me a powder for it, and plays the poticary; they call it flock-powder; they do so incorporate it to the cloth that it is wonderful to consider; truly, a goodly invention. O that so goodly wits should be so ill applied! They may well deceive the people, but they cannot deceive God."[1]

This course of sermons, preached by Latimer before the young king in the Lent terms of 1549 and 1550 (the sermon "on the Plough" was in 1548), constitute the chief glory of his life. They contain, as we have seen, a complete picture of the times, painted indeed in lurid colours, but they still remain among the most valuable documents of the time. They attracted, as indeed they could not fail to do, much attention, and were attended by large crowds of people. The preacher himself was keenly stirred by the corrupt state of society, his heart was full of his subject, and he expressed himself with an exceptional force and animation, adding to the glow and humanness of his pictures by little picturesque touches and humorous anecdotes, not the least entertaining being the occasional autobiographical details. It is not possible to refuse Latimer our admiration. The only pity is that he should occasionally have laid himself open to adverse criticism. The passages in which he refers to Lord Seymour cannot be justified, or even strongly defended. No doubt Lord Seymour was a scoundrel, and a thorough-going scoundrel, but that fact does not justify, though it may extenuate, Latimer's fierce denunciation of him after he was dead. Lord Seymour of Sudeley was a brother of the Protector, the Duke of Somerset, and a man of like

[1] *Sermons*, p. 138.

ambitions with himself. Bold, too, and regardless as to what means he used to attain his ends. He felt himself aggrieved by the fact that his brother had full power in the kingdom, while he himself occupied a subsidiary position; and by every means in his power he tried to change this state of affairs, and to press his own advantage, in hopes of gradually supplanting his brother. He had married Catherine Parr, the late king's widow, within a fortnight of Henry's death, and when she died, some short time after, he tried to marry the Princess Elizabeth, but the Council would have none of him. He was full of wild schemes, won for himself the sympathies of a certain proportion of the Lords, and had secret dealings and conspiracies with all manner of people. It appears to be pretty clear that he was conspiring against Somerset, who, on obtaining evidence of this, promptly had him arrested. His confederate, Sherington, who had earned the hatred of the nation by his debasing of the coinage, was also arrested, and confessed his guilt, implicating Seymour along with him. The admiral demanded an open trial, but Parliament decided on the more rapid process of attainder. With a show of justice, he was allowed to plead, but, after answering a few of the questions put to him, he refused to plead further, and was condemned and executed. This was in 1549.

It is very probable that the man richly deserved his fate, though it may be reasonably wondered why his brother did not intervene, or at least plead for him to Parliament. With his degree of guilt we are not concerned. But it is not easy to understand how

Latimer could be so strong in his arraignment of the one brother and his defence of the other. It is the only occasion on which he seems to occupy the position of the court preacher, for at all other times he is as strong in speaking candidly about the king and all authorities as about anyone in less dignified position. It has been maintained that he spoke at the instigation of Somerset, through whom he obtained certain details as to the latter days of Seymour, which he recounts in his sermons. His action is certainly in no way like himself, but, such as it was, it must be recorded. Had Seymour still been alive, there had been little to say against Latimer's animadversions, save possibly that they indicated a lack of taste on the part of the preacher; but his death, and the fashion of his death, puts a different aspect on the matter. "He was a man," said Latimer, "the farthest from the fear of God that ever I knew or heard of in England." "Surely he was a wicked man; the realm is well rid of him; it hath a treasure that he is gone." . . . "As touching the kind of his death, whether he be saved or no, I refer that to God only. He may, in the twinkling of an eye, save a man and turn his heart; and when a man hath two strokes with an axe, who can tell but that between two strokes he doth repent. But this I will say, that he died very dangerously, irksomely, horribly."[1] Then he goes on to tell of some of his many enormities. While a prisoner in the Tower, Seymour, it seems, had written two notes to the Princesses Elizabeth and Mary, urging them to conspire against the Protector. "When he was ready to lay his head

[1] *Sermons*, pp. 161, 163, 164.

upon the block, he turns unto the lieutenant's servant and saith: 'Bid my servant speed the thing that he wots of.' . . . What would he have done if he had lived still, that went about this gear, when he had laid his head on the block, at the end of his life?" Latimer had himself seen these notes, and was full of admiration and wonder at the great "subtilty" of Seymour in having contrived to write them, with a pen constructed of the aglet of a point plucked from his hose, and ink of most crafty workmanship. Then he goes on to recount a squalid tale of vice of a woman who had been undone by this Seymour—"a wanton woman, a naughty liver." " Peradventure this may seem a light matter, but surely it is a great matter; and he by unrepentance fell from evil to worse, and from worse to worst of all, till at length he was made a spectacle to all the world." There is nothing to be said in defence of Seymour in this matter, but it does seem a little uncalled for to rake up such a story about a man who at all events had paid a heavy price for his sins. "I have heard say," continues Latimer, "he was of the opinion that he believed not the immortality of the soul, and it might well appear by the taking of his death. But ye will say, What, ye slander, ye break charity. Nay, it is charity that I do. There can be no better use of him now than to warn others to beware of him."[1] That charity cannot be called very complete which holds up all the sins and faults of a man to the detestation of the public, without adding any extenuating qualifications. No man is altogether bad, and, blackguard though Seymour was, it seems gratuitous to have

[1] *Sermons*, pp. 164, 165.

enlarged on his wickedness to a public who were not specially inclined to admire him.

In another sermon Latimer is at pains to vindicate Parliament for passing the Act of Attainder.[1] "By this ye may perceive it is possible for a man to answer for himself and be arraigned at the bar, and nevertheless to have wrong. . . . So it is possible in a case for a man that hath in his absence attaintment to have right and no wrong. I will not say nay, but it is a good law for a man to answer for himself; this is reasonable, allowable, and good; and yet such an urgent cause may be, such a respect to a commonwealth, that a man may rightly be condemned in his absence. . . . In Parliament, although he were not there himself, any friend he had, had liberty to answer for him, frank and free. . . . There were in the Parliament, in both Houses, a great many learned men, conscionable men, wise men. When that man was attainted there, and they had liberty there to say nay to his attaintment if they would; sure I am the most allowed it, or else it could not have gone forward." Canon Dixon suggests that these sermons, which were published within two or three months of their delivery, may have gone forth as a sort of vindication of the Protector and Parliament.[2] Latimer says: "Some liken me to Doctor Shaw that preached at Paul's Cross, that King Edward's sons were bastards" (with the object of invalidating their title to the Crown). "An easy matter for one of the Council to do as Doctor Shaw did. . . . The Council needs not my lie for the defence of that that they do. . . . You will say this: the Parliament House are

[1] *Sermons*, pp. 181, 182.   [2] Dixon, iii. 13, note.

wiser than I am; you might leave them to the defence of themselves. . . . Yet have I spoken this of a good zeal and a good ground of the admiral's writing; I have not feigned nor lied one jot, I take God to witness. . . . Some say, preachers should not meddle with such matters; but did not our Saviour Jesus Christ meddle with matters of judgment when He spake of the wicked judge, to leave example to us to follow, to do the same."[1] Yet once again he returns to the same subject in one of the last sermons he preached before the young king. He was preaching on the subject of prayer, and wishing that all men would use it, as Christ had urged upon them to do. Without any special reason he diverged from his more general exhortation to make an attack on the late Lord Admiral. "I have heard say," he went on, "when that good queen that is gone" (Catherine Parr) "had ordained in her house daily prayer both before noon and afternoon, the admiral gets him out of the way, like a mole digging in the earth. He shall be Lot's wife to me as long as I live. He was, I heard say, a covetous man, a covetous man indeed; I would there were no more in England! He was, I heard say, an ambitious man; I would there were no more in England. He was, I heard say, a seditious man, a contemner of common prayer; I would there were no more in England. Well, he is gone."[2] We must, of course, remember that it was Latimer's method to seize hold on any contemporary incident or occurrence, and to take this as his text. But even remembering this his habit and custom, it is impossible not to feel a pang of disappointment that he

[1] *Sermons*, p. 184.   [2] *Ibid.* p. 228.

should, so far as he did, lower himself to blacken the character of a man who, however bad, had at least paid, to some extent, the penalty of his wickedness, and who was no longer alive to defend himself.

One very prevalent evil of the day has not been mentioned, but it was not ignored by the preacher—the terrible corruption of immorality, the dreadful commonness of adultery. As early as 1528 Sir Thomas More [1] had observed with respect to this sin in the reign of Henry: " We see ... not only the rich but the pore also, kepe open queues and live in open advoutry, without paiment or penaunce or anything almost ones sayd unto them." Latimer adds his witness to the same tale. " If it be true that is told it is marvel that it (London) doth not sink, and that the earth gapeth not and swalloweth it up. It is wonderful that the city of London doth suffer such whoredom unpunished. . . . There is some place in London, as they say 'immunity, impunity'; what should I call it? a privileged place for whoredom. The lord mayor hath nothing to do there, the sheriffs they cannot meddle with it, and the quest they do not inquire of it . . . and there is no reformation of it." [2] " There was never more lechery used in England than is at this day and maintained.[3] It is made but a laughing matter and a trifle; but it is a sad matter and an earnest matter; for lechery is a great sin. . . . There be such dicing houses also they say as hath not been wont to be, where young gentlemen dice away their thrift; and where dicing is, there are other follies also. For the love of God let remedy be had, let us wrestle

---

[1] *Works*, 249 (*Sermons*, p. 244).   [2] *Sermons*, p. 196.
[3] *Ibid.* p. 244.

and strive against sin. Men of England in times past when they would exercise themselves,—for we must needs have some recreation, our bodies cannot endure without some exercise,—they were wont to go abroad in the fields a-shooting, but now it is turned into glossing, gulling, and whoring within the house. The art of shooting hath been in times past much esteemed in this realm; it is a gift of God that He hath given us to excel all other nations withal . . . it is a goodly art, a wholesome kind of exercise and much commended in physic."[1] Apparently this "goodly art" had fallen into practical disuse, as indeed we have evidence in the Act for the maintaining of artillery. Latimer tells how his father used to exercise him in shooting as diligently as in any other lesson; he remarks on the great change in this custom in his own lifetime, and urges the magistrates to take some action in the matter, to stir men up to practise this excellent pastime rather than to indulge in their sensual and wicked passions.

As a rule, indeed, Latimer not only lashes the evil but tries to discover some remedy for it. He is no mere orator, but an earnest practical reformer. And while there were certain among his hearers who were stirred to wrath and indignation, there were yet others who heard gladly, who repented and changed their ways, some even offering restitution to those they had wronged. But the state of the country was very perilous. "Let the preacher preach till his tongue be worn to the stumps, nothing is amended. We have good statutes made for the commonwealth, as touching commons and inclosers; many meetings

[1] *Sermons*, pp. 196, 197.

and sessions, but in the end of the matter nothing cometh forth," nothing, that is, compared to what must be before the country could be restored to tranquillity and prosperity.

The sermon on covetousness, from which frequent quotation has been made, was the last preached by Latimer before the king (Lent 1550). But he was not silent. According to Augustus Bernher, his Swiss attendant and faithful friend, the man to whom we owe much for his loving gathering together and editing of his master's sermons, he preached twice every Sunday throughout the reign of Edward, with rare exceptions;[1] and there have been preserved a certain number of these sermons, preached in Lincolnshire, at Grimsthorpe Castle, the house of the Duchess of Suffolk, who is spoken of as a great professor and patroness of true religion and an excellent woman.[2] Whether before the king or the duchess, whether in London or Lincoln, the preacher's theme was ever the same; he always harped on the social evils prevalent everywhere, and called men to reform their ways and to practise their Christian principles. And, indeed, there was now, no less than before, need for this voice crying for reform. The Council, indeed, was mainly composed of men who nominally were of the reforming party, but in very truth many of them had no sort of religious principle, and only cared for their own advancement, for their own power, and not at all for the true good of the country. Somerset had fallen, and had expiated his offences on the scaffold, and the chief power was now in the hands of the Duke of Northumberland, hands very far from

[1] *Sermons*, p. 320.   [2] Strype, M. ii. i. 202.

clean. He showed himself severe indeed against all the supporters of Somerset, and was ready to visit their offences with heavy punishment; but the country was none the better, for he himself took advantage of his position to help himself to the public funds, and his family and friends to no small spoil. It is true that King Edward began to take a more active part in affairs, and showed that he had not been altogether unaffected by the many discourses against social evils to which he had listened during his young life. He appointed commissions of inquiry, and made various efforts after reform, but he did not live long enough to do much. He had never been strong, and it is not unlikely that the part he had to take in public affairs was too much for his weakly constitution. On the 6th of July 1553 he died, his last act being the formal disinheriting of his sisters in favour of Lady Jane Grey. This, of course, was done at the instigation of Northumberland, who felt that all his hopes depended on his securing the succession to his own household; and this he helped to accomplish by marrying his son to Lady Jane Grey, and persuading the king that on her succession depended the safety of the reformed religion. By threats or persuasions, but chiefly by the earnest appeals of the dying boy-king, many very important men, and among them the Archbishop of Canterbury, were induced to sign the paper drawn up by Northumberland, an act of folly to be bitterly repented and atoned for. It is not necessary to enter into details as to the manner in which Northumberland's plans were frustrated, and his unfortunate victim, Lady Jane, brought to a tragic end. Suffice it to say, Mary was proclaimed queen amidst the acclamations of the nation, who rallied round her as the daughter of Henry, and who were in no mind to submit any longer to Northumberland and his friends. He was no favourite, and Mary was her father's daughter. It was speedily manifest that her claim was acknowledged; she was queen by virtue of her father's will, and the deed left by the dying Edward was null and of no effect.

CHAPTER V

THE Protestant party had little to expect at the hands of Mary. An ardent Catholic by training, the circumstances of her early life had not been such as were likely to incline her to tolerance. It was hardly possible to expect that the daughter of Catherine of Aragon could feel anything but bitterness towards those who had caused such suffering to her mother. Politically she seemed at first inclined to leniency, though strongly advised to severity by Renard, the Spanish ambassador, who was one of her chief counsellors. His great desire was not reconciliation with Rome, but the establishment of Mary's position as queen and the strengthening of the friendly relations between England and Spain. Despite his urgency, however, Mary showed herself in no great haste to rid herself permanently of her gentle rival, Lady Jane. It would seem that she was only finally convinced of this necessity by the rising of Wyatt, some eight months after her accession. Then, indeed, she listened to the insistent advice of Renard and Gardiner, and consented to the execution of the youthful Lady Jane and her husband.

In religious matters, Mary's spirit was very different. Here she needed no stirring up, no inciting to vigorous action; on the contrary, Renaud, with his mind intent on the political crisis of the country, and seeing very clearly that the nation as a whole was far from inclined to return to allegiance to Rome, did his best to check and control Mary's zeal and ardour. She was, however, not unsupported, for she had the full sympathy and enthusiastic counsel of her cousin, Cardinal Pole, a man even more zealous than herself, if that were possible, in the cause of Rome, even more determined to haste and precipitancy in the matter of the restoration of the papal power. Her first measures were to restore the bishops who were favourable to the old religion, to sanction the restoration of the Roman mass, and to forbid all general preaching, granting a licence to those preachers only who were well known to be inclined to Rome. The alarm of the Protestants can easily be imagined. It was rumoured that Cranmer himself was so untrue to his principles as to have offered to "sing the Mass and Requiem at the burial of the king, either before the queen or at St. Paul's Church, or anywhere else, and that he had said or restored Mass in Canterbury." He hastened to publish a declaration denying the accusation, and maintaining the principles of the Prayer-Book and of Protestantism. Mary could forgive anything but heresy; Cranmer had signed the deed of Edward VI., willing away the crown from his sister, an act she might very well have resented and fairly enough have punished as treason, but she had to all appearance forgiven that, for the archbishop had been left undisturbed; but now her resentment was roused effectually, and he was committed to the Tower. The other Protestant preachers were either driven from the country by significant hints as to what might happen to them if they stayed in England, or were summoned to London and imprisoned. Among these latter was Latimer. The summons found him at Stamford in Warwickshire. He had some six hours' warning of the coming of the king's messenger, so that he might have escaped with no great difficulty had he so desired. But he was too far advanced in years to care about fleeing to another country; and, more than that, he thought it was his duty to witness for his God before the queen. When the pursuivant arrived, to his great astonishment, he found the old man calmly making ready for his journey, and when he told the object of his visit Latimer assured him he was "a welcome messenger to me. Be it known unto you and to all the world, that I go as willingly to London at this present, being called by my prince to render a reckoning of my doctrine, as ever I was at any place in the world. And I doubt not but that God, as He hath made me worthy to preach His word before two excellent princes, so will He able me to witness the same unto the third, either to her comfort, or discomfort eternally."[1] It seemed as if those in power wished to give the old man every chance of escape, for the pursuivant, when he had given over his letters, refused to wait for him, saying that he had his orders to this effect. Be this as it may, Latimer quietly submitted, and without haste or delay made his way up to London and appeared before the Council. As he passed through Smithfield he remarked that the place had long groaned for him, no

[1] Foxe, vii. 464.

doubt thinking in his heart that the time was close at hand when he should witness on that spot for the honesty of his convictions. After some little questioning, the Council declared him to be a seditious person, and he was cast into the Tower, where he was treated with considerable rigour, being "ordered into close prison, and allowed no comforts." He was an old man now, and the confinement and the hardships of his position told upon him. Then the wintry weather came on; he suffered considerably from the cold of his room, for even in the frost he had no fire —a great deprivation for an old man. But he made no complaint beyond sending the lieutenant a message that if he did not look better to him, perchance he would deceive him. The lieutenant, so the story goes,[1] hurried to his prisoner to see what he meant, thinking he had devised some plan of escape. "Yea, so I said," quoth he, "for you look I think that I should burn; but except you let me have some fire, I am like to deceive your expectation, for I am like here to starve for cold." Probably the lieutenant was moved to pity the old man's condition, for we hear no more of the cold; it does not appear that he was really much worse in bodily condition when he left the Tower than when he entered, and it is incredible that he should have lingered on in a cold, comfortless room for seven weary months and yet have come out scathless.

After Wyatt's rebellion the Tower was so crowded that Cranmer, Ridley, Latimer, and Bradford were confined in one room, and that not a very large one.[2] They were not, however, disposed to grumble at an

[1] Foxe, vii. 464.   [2] Strype, "Cranmer," i. 463.

arrangement which permitted them to take counsel together and to encourage one another in their common faith. They spent great part of their time in carefully re-reading the New Testament, searching for any proofs of the Romish doctrine of the corporal presence, "but after all, they could find no presence but a spiritual, nor that the Mass was any sacrifice for sin."

For a time at least Mary showed no great haste to be rid of these particular heretics; possibly she thought a prolonged sojourn in the Tower might put so great a strain on their principles as to make them more ready to abandon them. At all events, there they lay until the spring of the following year, when they were removed to the prison of Bocardo in Oxford,[1] being sent there that they might stand their trial, or the farce of a trial. Already the clergy had met at Westminster, and appointed a Commission to meet at Oxford, where they summoned the three chief Protestants, Cranmer, Latimer, and Ridley, to dispute certain questions of religion with Weston, the Dean of Westminster, and various other members of Convocation, aided by a deputation from Cambridge, the university to which all three heretics belonged.[2] It would seem to have been an illegàl and irregular action to try bishops on such a charge as this by any but their peers; but Convocation entirely disregarded the common law and practice, no one of the deputation sent by them being above the rank of presbyter. But indeed that mattered very little. The trial was no real one, for the accused

[1] March 8, 1554.
[2] Strype, "Cranmer," i. pp. 479, 480.

were practically judged beforehand; there can be
no doubt that the queen and the leaders of the
Romish party thought their cause would be stronger
were the leaders of the reforming party out of
the way, and Cranmer, Ridley, and Latimer were
regarded as the heads and mainsprings of the reforming movement.

In Oxford they were lodged in the prison of
Bocardo, beside St. Michael's Church in the Cornmarket, but they were no longer allowed to be
together or to consult with one another, save that
occasionally they were permitted to dine together in
the prison. In the matter of food they seem to have
been very well treated, so far as we can judge by the
bill of fare preserved for us by Strype.[1] " October 1.—
Bread and ale, 2d.; oysters, 1d.; butter, 2d.; eggs, 2d.;
ling, 8d.; fresh salmon, 10d.; wine, 3d.; cheese and
pears, 2d.—total, 2s. 6d." For prison fare this cannot
be counted very poor feeding. Two bailiffs of the city
were held responsible for the cost of their keep, as
also for the fagots, chains, posts, and all the other
expenses of their burning,[2] and these bailiffs found
themselves considerably out of pocket, as is evident
from their petition to the bishops, some ten years
later, in which they pointed out that they had
expended a very considerable sum, that their case
was very miserable, and their debt just. Apparently
money had been sent to Oxford to pay for the
prisoners' keep, but somehow or another it was
embezzled. Latimer complains that they were kept
very strictly in the prison. "No man might come
at him to supply him in his needs; no, not so much

[1] Strype, "Cranmer," i. p. 562.   [2] *Ibid.*

as to mend his hose, though he had but one pair."[1] It is hard to understand how he occupied himself during the long time that he lay in prison, for he has left almost no writings. There is a short treatise composed by him along with Ridley, and there are three letters, but beyond these there is nothing. The letters, too, convey very little—one is a mere note of thanks to a Mrs. Wilkinson, who had shown him some kindness while he was in prison; another, a general exhortation to all unfeigned lovers of God's truth to remain constant to their faith; while the third is a letter of encouragement and counsel to a brother whose faith was failing him. In truth Latimer was not a writer, and had no special literary gifts. He was pre-eminently a speaker, a preacher to men, and no doubt he recognised that his powers did not lie in the direction of writing, and therefore left that to Ridley and Cranmer, while he himself spent long hours in reading and re-reading his well-loved New Testament. He deliberately "read through the Testament seven times, and could never find there neither flesh, blood, nor bones, nor this word transubstantiation." He had all his life been constant in prayer, and now in these last days he spent more time than ever on his knees, sometimes kneeling for so long that he was not able to rise without help. It is not without interest that we learn from Bernher the chief subjects of his prayer.[2] First he desired that he might have grace to be firm to the end, that God would give him strength to suffer any kind of cruel death rather than prove false to the

---

[1] Strype, M. iii. i. 376.
[2] Bernher, *Sermons*, p. 322.

belief that was in his heart. He was by no means too confident of himself, knowing that he was old and weak, and shrinking from fresh bodily suffering, and so it was for strength and courage that he most earnestly and constantly prayed. Next, he prayed for the establishment and restoration of the true gospel in England; and this he "did so inculcate and beat into the ears of the Lord God as though he had seen God before him, and spoke unto Him face to face." His third prayer was for the Princess Elizabeth, whom he constantly brought before God by name, looking to her to be a "comfort to the comfortless realm of England." In the absence of any other information about his last months, we cannot but be grateful to Bernher for these details.

The Commission deputed to examine the three heretics was composed of ten members of Convocation, besides the President Dr. Weston, the Vice-Chancellor, and a certain number of professors and doctors, representing the university, and joined to these was a deputation of seven Cambridge men, appointed by the Senate of that university, "not so much to dispute points so professedly orthodox," as to vindicate the university from any seeming approbation of Cranmer and Latimer.[1] Weston, the President, was regarded as a man of some learning, but was not distinguished by any devoutness of character, and his unscrupulous determination that the three bishops should be got rid of is clearly shown in his speech in Convocation, when it was objected that there was as yet no law of the land by which they could be condemned. "It forceth not

[1] Strype, "Cranmer," i. 480.

for a law, he said; we have commission to proceed with them. When they be despatched let their friends sue the law."[1] From such a man little could be expected by the reformers. Latimer, whose boldness was not decreased by the infirmities of age, did not scruple in his address to express his great surprise that Weston should sit in judgment on him and the others. "I never saw him before; and I had not thought he had been so great a clerk.[2] For in all King Edward's time he was a curate beside Bishopsgate, and held him well content to feed his parishioners with the doctrine that he now calleth heresy, and is sent from the queen to judge us of the same." Possibly Weston was irritated by this plain speaking, at all events he showed no sympathy or respect for the old man, but with bitter jibes did his best most unfairly to misrepresent the reformers and their opinions. "Like a sort of apes, they could not tell which way to turn their tails, looking one day west and another day east, one that way and another this way. They will be like, they say, to the apostles, they will have no churches. A hovel is good enough for them. They come to the communion with no reverence. They get them a tankard, and one saith, I drink and I am thankful. The more joy of thee, saith another." Such was the man who presided over this Commission, which now proceeded to sit in judgment on the three reformers. They met in St. Mary's, the University Church, and having formally read the letters constituting them a Commission, and provided themselves with three public

[1] Dixon, iv. 176, quoting from Hooper.
[2] Dispute at Oxford, *Remains*, p. 260.

notaries, they proceeded solemnly to celebrate the Mass of the Holy Ghost, then, in accordance with the university custom, they marched through the town in procession to Christ Church, where an anthem was sung and a collect read; they then returned to St. Mary's, took their seats in the choir, and summoned before them the arch-heretic, the once all-powerful and still formidable archbishop, Cranmer. The sight must have been an impressive one; the Commission, dressed in their scarlet robes of office, sitting in dignified state in the beautiful choir of St. Mary's stately church, faced by the solitary figure of the archbishop, staff in hand.[1] On entering he "gave them great reverence," but refused to sit on the stool offered to him.[2] Weston began proceedings with a discourse upon the desirability of unity in the Church, and his mission from the queen to recover the archbishop to that unity. Convocation had drawn up certain articles, and they desired him to subscribe. In answer, Cranmer expressed his own desire for unity, "so it were in Christ, and according to the Church of God." He then read over the articles submitted to him, expressed his opinion that they were not in accordance with God's word, but prayed to be permitted to consider them for the night. It was agreed that he should give his opinion of them that night, and that afterwards there should be open discussion of all disputed points, he being supplied with any books he should desire. Then he was taken back to Bocardo, leaving behind him a wonderful impression of humility and modesty, so great "that many masters of art who were not of his mind could not forbear

[1] Dixon, iv. 184.   [2] Strype, "Cranmer," i. 481.

weeping.[1] Ridley was next brought in, and he spoke in the same strain as Cranmer, desiring time for consideration, and expressing a readiness to dispute.

Last of all they brought in old Latimer, of whose appearance Strype gives us a full and detailed description. "He held a hat in his hand, he had a kerchief on his head, and upon it a night-cap or two, and a great cap such as townsmen used with two broad flaps to button under his chin; an old threadbare Bristow freez gown, girded to his body with a penny leather girdle, at which hanged by a long string of leather his Testament; and his spectacles without case hanging about his neck upon his breast."[2] To him, as to the others, Weston gave the articles, and asked for his answer to them. Latimer, in reply, explained that he did believe in a presence in the sacrament, but not such an one as was expressed in the articles.[3] He would shortly give them a reply to the articles, but he could not bear a dispute, for he was old and infirm, and his memory was no longer strong. This was on the Saturday. They were all taken back to Bocardo, and left there to consider the articles until the Monday, when they were again summoned to appear before the Commission.

The questions put to them, on the answers to which depended their lives, were these—

1. In the Sacrament of the altar, by virtue of God's Word pronounced by the priest, there is really the true and natural body of Christ present, which was conceived of the Virgin Mary, under the kinds of bread and wine; and in like manner His blood.

[1] Strype, "Cranmer," i. 482.   [2] *Ibid.* 483.   [3] *Ibid.*

2. After the consecration there remaineth no substance of bread and wine, nor any other substance but the substance of Christ, God, and man.

3. In the Mass there is the life-giving sacrifice of the Church, which is propitiatory for the sins as well of the quick as the dead.[1]

It was the old doctrine of the papists, set forth with all clearness for the undoing of the three ecclesiastics.

On the Monday the Commission sat again, this time in the divinity schools, and, as had been previously arranged, Cranmer was given an opportunity to dispute the articles. He spoke with great calmness and with the respectful modesty which rarely forsook him, but his opponents were only eager to silence him; they clamoured against him with "such noise and crying out that his mild voice could not be heard." In Ridley's account of the so-called disputation he says he "never in all his life saw or heard anything carried more vainly and tumultuously: he could not have thought that there could have been found among Englishmen any persons, honoured with degrees in learning, that willingly could allow of such vanities, more fit for the stage than the schools. . . . When he studied at Paris, he remembered what clamours were used in the Sorbon, where popery chiefly reigned; but that was a kind of modesty in comparison of this thrasonical ostentation. Whence he concluded very truly that they fought not for the sincere truth in this Conference, and for nothing but vain glory."[2] On Wednesday the 18th of April,

[1] M. iii. i. 75 (in Latin).
[2] Strype, "Cranmer," i. 485.

Latimer was in his turn brought before the Commission, but he was not allowed to read what he had written, the prolocutor reading part of it and then proceeding to the disputation. There was no consideration for the old man; he was taunted and laughed at, hissed and scorned, even as Cranmer and Ridley had been. He was very faint and sick, and begged Weston to be good to him as an old man, reminding him that he too might once be old and feeble. He also asked that he might be permitted to speak in English, as for some twenty years he had not much used the Latin tongue. Weston then proceeded to question him in respect to the articles, showing him scant courtesy and speaking lightly of the opinions generally held by the reformers. Latimer again expressed himself as unwilling, and unfit, by reason of his great age to engage in formal disputation, and desired only that he might be permitted to read the declaration he had written out. This, however, he was not suffered to do, but he was badgered with many questions, and made to express himself on the articles. "Disputation," he said, "requireth a good memory. My memory is gone clean and marvellously weakened and never the better for the prison." He was clear that the presence of Christ in the Mass was a spiritual one; and when one of the disputants sought to prove to him from certain words of Hilary, that in very truth Christ was present in His bodily substance, he made answer in the words of Melancthon: "If the doctors had foreseen that they should have been so taken in this controversy, they would have written more plainly." He admitted freely that it was only of late years that his mind had been clear on the sacrament: he had long sought for the truth, and had carefully read and read the Scriptures, with the one intent of finding the true doctrine; for some seven years he had been of his present mind and had been strongly confirmed in his judgment by Cranmer's book, and indeed if he could but remember all contained therein he would not fear to answer any man in the matter.

After much questioning, mocking, and scorning, Weston brought the proceedings to an end in a coarse speech, with loud mocking at the reformers as flingbrains and flightheads, and exhorting Latimer to recant and trust to the queen's mercy. Two days after, the three bishops were once more called before the Commission, and asked whether they would subscribe the articles. Weston declared that they had been overcome in disputation, but they boldly denied this, and all three firmly expressed their resolve to stand by what they had said. Sentence was read over them; they were no longer members of the Church, but were condemned as heretics. The reading of the sentence was interrupted for a minute while they were asked once more if they would not turn. They bade read on in the name of God, and so they were condemned and sent back to prison. Cranmer appealed to the just judgment of God, trusting to be present with Him in heaven. Ridley said calmly that the sentence would but send them the sooner thither, where else they hoped to go; while Latimer solemnly thanked God that his life had been prolonged so that he might glorify God by this kind of death.

But their time to die was not yet come. This was

in April, and as yet the queen had not determined on stamping out heresy by fear of the stake. They were doomed to lie in Bocardo till the following September, and then once more to be examined and warned and exhorted before the final witness to their faith. The return to prison and the long lingering there must have been peculiarly trying to them all. They were lodged apart. "We were separated, so that none of us knoweth what the other did."[1] Their servants were discharged, that they might not have any communication with one another, or receive news from the outer world. But though they were no longer men of power and position, they were not altogether deserted. Supplies of meat, money, and shirts were sent to them from London, not only by their friends, of whom they had many, but by some who were strangers to them and who pitied their sad state, contrasting so strongly as it did with their former high place. Strangely enough the universities were with one accord against them. They had no sympathy at all from the scholars: Oxford as well as Cambridge was all for the old religion. Ridley in a letter to Bradford expressed his great surprise at this undoubted fact, wondering exceedingly that among so many never yet scholar offered any of them any manner of favour. Such comforts as reached them they had in common, but they were obtained in spite of, not through the kindness of the university.

In his appearance before the Commission in September, Latimer asks how they can reasonably look for learning at his hands, one who for so long

[1] Strype, "Cranmer," i. 945.

had been kept without books, "the bare walls my library—so long in prison, without book or pen or ink; and now you let me loose to come and answer to articles."

The queen had been very much occupied with her husband, and with the negotiations concerning the return to England of her cousin, Reginald Pole, in the character of pope's legate. Pole was a man of learning and of many excellent qualities, chief among which, in the mind of the queen, was his devotion to the cause of the papacy. But he was not a strong man, not a man for troubled times; he lacked the decision and resolution necessary for a leader. Latimer had recognised his learning and his good qualities, and had mourned over his devotion to Rome. "I never remember that man," he said, "but with a heavy heart; a witty man, a learned man, a man of a noble house; so in favour that if he had tarried in the realm and would have conformed himself to the king's proceedings, I heard say, and I believe it verily, he had been Bishop of York at this day, and he would have done much good in that part of the realm; for those quarters have always had need of learned men and a preaching prelate. A thing to be much lamented that such a man should take such a way. . . . He goeth about to dissuade the king from his supremacy. In his persuasions he is very homely, very quick, and sharp with the king."[1] With all his anxiety to reconcile the country to Rome, Pole at first showed no desire to proceed to extremities with the heretics. When the bishops and clergy waited on him at Lambeth (Jan. 1554), he exhorted them all to return

[1] *Sermons*, p. 174.

to their charges and to strive their utmost by mild persuasion and gentleness, rather than by rigour and severity, to bring their flocks back to the old faith.[1] It is not clear whether in truth he would, if left to himself, have persevered in these his professed purposes of mildness and gentleness. There were others besides Pole at the queen's side, urging her on to a thorough extirpation not only of heresy but of the heretics. It may very well be that Pole's gentler counsels were overborne by the stronger, fiercer spirits he had to deal with, and that he yielded against his better judgment to the pursuing zeal of Mary. Be that as it may, the case of the reformers in the year 1555 became increasingly grave and serious. In every parish inquiry was made as to those who were disaffected to Rome, any who did not attend mass were to be brought before the justices, and if they would not conform, were to be sent to prison. In every parish there were to be one or more secret informers to give notice of all who did not go to mass or who spoke against the old superstitions. Many of the professors of the reformed religion left the country and sought refuge abroad, while the prisons were crowded with those haled before the justices and accused by the informers.

The queen was distracted with sorrow, and disappointed. Her husband, whom she loved with all the intensity of her narrow soul, cared not a jot for her, and she was beginning to perceive his coldness. Her hopes for a son, who would bring husband and wife together, and attach to them the loyalty of the nation,

[1] Dixon, iv. 326.

had come to nought. In bitterness of soul, she thought that Heaven was angry with her because she had not shown sufficient zeal for religion,[1] and, convinced, that nothing could succeed prosperously with her while any heretics remained in her kingdom, she instituted fresh and severer measures against them. It is not improbable that these superstitious ideas were fostered and strengthened by those among her counsellors who sympathised with her religious views, and who at the same time distrusted and detested certain of the reformers, and were keenly desirous of their death. However this may be, the fate of Ridley and Latimer, among others, was now decided. Cranmer was to linger yet awhile in prison, and to go through many trying passages, before his final testimony was given; but the other two were now to pass through their fiery trial. In September 1555 Ridley and Latimer were once more called before commissioners, this time presided over by the Bishop of Lincoln, who was careful to explain that he and the others were sitting in judgment on the bishops, in virtue of a Commission granted them by Pole, as pope's legate.[2] It must have been bitter hearing for the reformers, as confirming the news that had penetrated to their prisons, that for the time being the cause of reform was lost, and the papacy once more in power.

As Latimer passed from the prison to the divinity schools, where sat the commissioners, he was hustled and jostled by the crowd, in such fashion that he was not a little hurt, and, being old and frail, he was in poor condition when he reached the hall. To add to

[1] Strype, "Cranmer," i. 528.
[2] Foxe, vii. 518.

his discomfort, he was kept waiting for some time outside the schools, "gazing at the cold walls, with great hurt to his old age." This, however, was not done purposely, and the Bishop of Lincoln expressed his great sorrow that he had been brought so soon from the prison, and explained that it was the bailiff's fault. He then proceeded "gently to exhort" the old bishop to return to the unity of the Church, and to acknowledge his errors and false assertions, in which case, according to the commission from the legate, they would grant him the benefit of absolution; but otherwise, they must, loth though they were to do so, proceed to carry out the second part of the mission laid on them; not to condemn him—that they would leave to the temporal sword—but to cut him off as a rotten member of the Church and commit him to the temporal judges. Latimer in his reply admitted the gentle courtesy with which the bishop addressed him, but stoutly defended himself against the admission that the Roman Church and the Catholic Church were one. He gave clear answer to all the questions put to him, but protested, and called the notaries to witness to his protestation, that by so answering he did not for a moment acknowledge the authority of the pope of Rome, for he was the queen's subject and could not serve two masters. As to the doctrine of the sacrament, "the bread is still bread, and the wine still wine, for the change is not in the nature but in the dignity." To all the articles he gave much the same answers as before, as indeed was fully anticipated. The bishop declared that his assertions were not, however, to be taken as final, that he must appear again, and begged him to ponder afresh all these things until the morrow. Latimer, exhausted by these endless and fruitless questionings, begged not to be troubled on the morrow—"for I am at a point; you shall give me respite in vain." There was no remedy. He was handed over to the mayor to appear next morning at eight in St. Mary's Church.

The next day, after Ridley had been interviewed and condemned, Latimer was summoned. But first, "the cloth which lay on the table whereat Master Ridley stood was removed because Latimer had never had the degree of a doctor as Master Ridley had." Little did Latimer care. Noting the absence of the cloth, he took his old felt hat and put it under his elbows while he stood his questioning. It was but a repetition of the day before. The articles were again repeated, and Latimer, once again protesting that by replying he did not acknowledge the pope's authority, answered as before. Then the Bishop of Lincoln exhorted him to revoke, but he answered that he neither could nor would deny his Master Christ and His verity; whereupon the bishop read his condemnation and his sentence, and the session was broken up, Latimer adding his protest, and desiring that he might appeal to the next General Council. The bishop was well content, but said it would be a long season before such a convocation as he meant would be called. The crowd at the door of the church was so great and so eager that it was very difficult to make way, and the bishop feared that Latimer might again be hurt. He showed what care and consideration he could, bidding the crowd disperse, and urging the mayor, into whose charge he had committed the prisoner, to wait till the streets were quiet before the old man passed through them.

For yet another fortnight the condemned bishops lay in prison, awaiting the summons to their execution. They were not even yet free from well-meant but irritating questionings and persuasions. The legate thought they might even yet be turned from their heresies, thinking that as they had not been all their lives but only for a few years fully convinced of these opinions for which they were to suffer, they could not therefore be immoveably fixed in them. He did not realise that though it was but seven years since full conviction had come to them, the whole trend of their thought had all along been in this one direction, that their convictions were the result of earnest, strenuous, self-devoted lives, and were not to be lightly shaken.

The legate could hardly be blamed, if he were honestly convinced of his own point of view, in continuing to the very last to try his best to persuade them to recant; none the less are our sympathies aroused by the picture of the two bishops, after all the questioning and discussing to which they had been subjected, worried and irritated in their last few days by the constant and unremitting efforts of Soto, the Spanish friar, whose task it was to try to persuade them to recant. The one refused to see him; on the other he made not the least impression.

At last, on 16th October 1555, they were led out to be burnt; Cranmer,[1] his heart sad within him, watching the little procession from his window in the prison tower. Ridley was neatly dressed in a furred black

[1] Strype, "Cranmer," i. 529. Foxe, *Acts*, etc. vii. 548, does not agree with this.

gown with a fur tippet round his neck; Latimer in his old cloak, covering a shroud. "Be of good comfort, Master Ridley, and play the man. We shall this day light such a candle, by God's grace, in England, as I trust shall never be put out!"[1]

Dr. Smith, sometime master of Whittington College, preached the customary sermon at the stake. Latimer may have called to mind the former occasion when he preached and Forest suffered. The subject of the discourse was, of course, the character and tenets of the two bishops; Smith did his best to belittle them, as it was his business to do. A certain man, Dorman, remarked that bags of gunpowder had been provided to put the martyrs the sooner out of pain. This was not as it should be, he thought. "This agreeth not with the martyrdom of Polycarp." Most men will incline to agree with Dean Noel, who rebuked the speaker for thoughts of severity and apparent joy in the sufferings of the martyrs, adding that Ignatius said he would provoke and anger the beasts that they might more speedily devour him, and why not provoke the heat of the fire as well.[2] Ridley was long of dying, and suffered horribly, but Latimer's feeble frame soon succumbed.[3] As the faggots were heaped around him, and all was set ready, "he raised his eyes to heaven" with an amiable and comfortable countenance, saying these words, "God is faithful which doth not suffer us to be tempted above our strength." In a moment the gunpowder exploded and his sufferings were over.[4]

He made his mistakes, he was impulsive and hasty,

[1] Foxe, vii. 550. [2] Strype, M. iii. i. 381, 387.
[3] Foxe, vii. 550. [4] Dixon, iv. 438.

but to say this is only to say that he had the defects of his qualities. Honest and sincere, simple and straightforward, and dowered with the rare gift of oratory, he spoke straight to the hearts of the people, and not only by his death but by the bright example of his life, he showed himself a true servant, a loyal soldier of his Lord and Master. "Did there ever any man flourish, I say not in England only, but in any nation in the world, after the apostles, who preached the gospel more sincerely, purely, and honestly than Hugh Latimer."[1]

[1] Strype, M. iii. i. 376.

INDEX

ACT of the Six Articles, opinions about, 104.
Articles, the Six, 101.
    the Ten, 87.

BAGGARD, Chancellor of Diocese of Worcester, 46.
    Benefice bestowed on, 65.
Baynton, Sir Edward, letter from Latimer to, 34, 37–39, 41.
Bernher, Augustine, 110, 158.
Bilney, Thomas, 12.
Bishops, appointment of reforming, by Henry VIII., 60.
Bishops' Book, 65, 89–91.
Bocardo, 156, 166.
Bradford, Rodolph, 65, 156, 166.
Bristol, Latimer preaches at, 46–52.
Buckmaster, Dr., Vice-Chancellor of Cambridge, 30.
Butts, Dr., and Latimer, 29, 34.

CAMBRIDGE, New Learning at, 7.
    Latimer goes to, 6.
Catherine of Aragon, divorce of, 22, etc.
Chantries, confiscation of property of, 129.
Chapuys, French Ambassador, 52.
Cranmer, 25, 52, 53, 78, 79, 89, 91, 93, 94, 99, 100, 101, 102, 103, 108, 111, 112, 114, 150, 153, 156, 158, 161, 172.
Convocation of 1536, 73, etc.
Cromwell, 6, 51, 65, 66, 77, 81, 82, 84, 86, 91, 99, 100.

EDWARD VI., 113, 150.
Elizabeth, Princess, 159.
Erasmus at Cambridge, 7.

FISHER, Bishop of Rochester, 20, 59.
Forest, Friar, 71, etc., 173.
Fox, Edward, Provost of King's College, Cambridge, 20, 25.

GARDINER, Master of Trinity Hall, Cambridge, 25, 27, 89.
Grey, Lady Jane, 150, 152.

HALES, blood of, 85.
Hales, John, 120, 128, etc.
Henry VIII., 92, 104, 105, 107, 110.
Hubberdine, opponent of Latimer at Bristol, 46–52.
Hylsey, John, Prior of the Dominicans in Bristol, his attitude to Latimer, 48, 49.

KING'S Book, 110, etc.
Kingston, West, Wiltshire, 34.

LATIMER—
    Birth, 4.
    Family, 4, 5.
    Education, 6.
    Fellow of Clare Hall, 6.
    Bachelor of Divinity, 6.
    Relations to the New Learning, 9, etc.
    Scholarship, 10.
    Turns to the Reformed opinions, 11.
    Sermons on the Card, 14, etc.

timer—*continued*.
  Relations with Bishop West, 18, etc.
  Relations with Wolsey, 20.
  And the divorce of Catherine of Aragon, 27.
  On the Commission on heretical books, 30.
  Letter to Henry VIII. on reading of Scripture, 32.
  Appointed to parish of West Kingston, 34.
  Letter on his work in his parish, 35.
  Complaints of him in the West, 36, etc.
  Cited before Bishop of London, 40.
  Cited to London and committed to prison, 44.
  Subscribes Articles, 44, etc.
  Sermons at Bristol, 46, etc.
  Commission of inquiry with regard to sermons at Bristol, 51.
  Report of Chapuys, presumably about, 52.
  Preaches again before Henry VIII., 53.
  Charge of sedition against, 54, etc.
  Appointed Bishop of Worcester, 56.
  Visitation of diocese, 61, etc.
  Injunctions issued by Latimer to diocese, 61.
  Complaints of the appointments he made, 64.
  And the monks, 66.
  Sermons at Paul's Cross against the clergy, etc., 68, etc.
  And the execution of Friar Forest, 71, etc.
  Sermons at opening of Convocation, 1536, 73, etc.
  And the suppression of the monasteries, 79, etc.
  And the Pilgrimage of Grace, 81, etc.
  And relics, 85, etc.
  And the Bishops' Book, 89-92.

Latimer—*continued*.
  Preaches in London in accordance with Monmouth's will, 97.
  And the Six Articles, 103.
  Retires from the bishopric of Worcester, 103.
  His position in the reign of Edward VI., 114, etc.
  Sermons during the reign, 115, etc.
  ,, on justice, 119, 136, 137.
  ,, on enhancement of rents, 121.
  ,, on covetousness, 123.
  ,, on enclosures, 126.
  ,, on regrating, 127.
  ,, on the London burgesses, 132.
  ,, on lack of charity for poor scholars at the universities, 133.
  ,, on want of education in the nobility, 133.
  ,, on the low state of the universities, 135.
  ,, on secular employments of ecclesiastics, 138.
  ,, on frauds in the manufacture of cloth, 140.
  ,, in reference to Lord Seymour of Sudeley, 141-147.
  ,, on the commonness of gross immorality, 147.
  ,, on neglect of archery and other manly exercises, 148.
  Committed to the Tower, 154.
  Sent to Oxford, and lodged in Bocardo, 156.
  Treatment in prison, 157.
  Before the Commission of Convocation, 159-166.
  Dress before the Commission, 162.

INDEX

Latimer—*continued*.
    Questions put to Latimer, Cranmer, and Ridley by the Commission, 162.
    On Cardinal Pole, 167.
    Before the second Commission, 169–172.
    Execution, 172–174.

MALVERN Priory, 68, 80.
Marillac, French Ambassador, 105.
Mary, Queen, 151, 152, 153, 156, 167, 168.
Melancthon, letter to Henry VIII., 107.
Monasteries, suppression of, 78, etc.
Monmouth, Humphrey, 97, etc.

NORTHUMBERLAND, Duke of, Protector, 131, 149, 150, 151.

PILGRIMAGE of Grace, 81, etc.
Pole, Cardinal, 153, 167, 168.

RENARD, Spanish Ambassador, 152.

Ridley, 156, 158, 162, 163, 166, 169, 171, 173.

ST. MARY'S CHURCH, Oxford, 161.
Seymour of Sudeley, Lord, 141–147.
Shaxton, Bishop of Salisbury, 60, 89, 103, 107.
Social condition of England under Edward VI., ch. iv.
Somerset, Duke of, 113, 114, 119, 131.
Suffolk, Duchess of, 149.

UNIVERSITIES—
    Consulted about divorce of Catherine of Aragon, 25, etc.
    Attitude of, to Latimer at time of his final imprisonment, 166.
    Condition of, under Edward VI., 133, etc.

WARHAM, Archbishop, and the New Learning, 7.
Weston, 159–165.
White, Dr., Bishop of Lincoln, 169–171.

www.ingramcontent.com/pod-product-compliance
Lightning Source LLC
Chambersburg PA
CBHW072133160426
43197CB00012B/2090